Advertising Campaign

Authored By:

Louis Rubin

Researched by the Staff of:
Wealth Achievers, Inc.

List of Advisories

PREFACE

In the Modern Business Texts the study of advertising is divided into three parts. First, in the Text on "Marketing and Merchandising," there is a complete presentation of the things that have to be considered by anyone who has anything to market before he sends out his salesmen or prepares his advertising.
That Text treats of the plan behind the campaign. After a manufacturer or dealer has studied the things that must precede any selling campaign—trade relations, the product, the market and the methods of reaching the market—he decides to use either personal salesmanship or advertising, or both, to sell his goods. The Text on "Advertising Principles" shows what advertising can do for his business, guides him in choosing the right advertising appeal and treats of what may be called the technique of advertising, writing the copy, preparing the illustrations and getting the advertisement before the public.

There is much more to advertising, however, than the making of a preliminary study and the writing of advertisements. The advertiser has to consider problems of organization, methods of identifying his goods, his relation with agencies, the selecting of mediums, distribution, dealer cooperation and a host of other things, all of which have an important part in the complete campaign. The present Text deals with the many essential parts of an advertising campaign which have not been considered in preceding Texts in the Modern Business Series. It gathers all the diverse considerations of the advertisers, shows their relation one to another and binds them into a unified whole. Throughout the Text the point of view is chiefly that of the manufacturer, because the manufacturer's advertising campaign is inclusive of all advertising problems—his dealers' as well as his own. Most of the subjects treated, therefore, will be of interest to the dealer as well as to the manufacturer. MAC MARTIN

ADVISORY 1

THE PURPOSE OF THE CAMPAIGN

1. *The struggle of business.* The word campaign signifies carefully planned and carefully coordinated effort. Its significance in war and in business is the same. The advertising campaign includes everything done by an advertiser to promote sales thru publicity, all planned in advance, and every part is designed to fit into the other parts so that there will be no conflicting effort, no friction—simply a smoothly running machine directed toward the goal of increased sales.

2. *The campaign a modern development.* The idea of uniting all the advertising of an organization into a strongly centered campaign is one of the latest developments of modern business. Thirty years ago an advertisement was an advertisement. It was thought of as nothing more than a brief announcement on paper. Advertisements were seldom changed. There was seldom a single underlying thought drawing together all parts of the publicity of a business. Today we find remarkable examples of unity. While there is more variation in copy and more change in advertisements than there used to be, the same purpose and the same ideas run thru all the publicity of an advertiser. We find advertisers creating an atmosphere around themselves and their goods which is the same in each advertising medium.

A typical example is that of Cluett, Peabody and Company, manufacturer of Arrow Collars and Arrow Shirts. The style of lettering used for the words "Arrow Collars" is the same in all advertisements. There is a similarity in the style of illustrations and in the tone of the copy. This is noticeable whether the advertisement appears in a magazine, on a streetcar card, or on a window display. The same illustrations are used in different forms, sometimes with a group of figures and sometimes with a single figure, in street-car cards, posters, window cards, and in every one of the other varied forms of advertising which the company uses. There is a unity of impression, a unity of purpose. Each advertisement supports its fellows. Each is a part of a complete campaign.

3. *Objects of campaigns.* While thirty years ago most advertising was thought of merely as general publicity, today every advertising campaign is backed by a definite purpose for the accomplishment of a specific object. We have begun to know why we advertise. Some campaigns are purely educational; others are purely competitive. Occasionally we find a campaign which seems to have no close relation to the promotion of the business of the advertiser. The *Literary Digest* spent thousands of dollars in full page advertisements in the leading newspapers of the country to raise money for the starving children of central and southeastern Europe. The practical man asks: "What does the *Literary Digest* get out of it ?" The Literary Digest gets a valuable list of possible subscribers and a certain amount of prestige thru being associated with a worthy enterprise.

A manufacturer of tarred roofing conducts an advertising campaign for the sale of bird houses at cost, and one asks, "What does this manufacturer of roofing obtain by such advertising?" While he obtains the same sort of prestige secured by the *Literary Digest* in his bird club advertising, he also has the satisfaction of knowing that he is sampling. his roofing, from which the bird boxes are made, to all the individuals purchasing these boxes.

These illustrations demonstrate the truth of the old adage that there are more ways than one to kill a cat. In each case there was a specific object for the campaign, though at first glance that object may seem to have had little to do with the business of the advertiser. The motive behind the effort remains in the back ground. The promotion of the advertiser's business was no less attained because the means were indirect.

In these days it is not enough to advertise just for the purpose of selling goods. The merchandising plan which is the foundation of the advertising must first be carefully studied. This will determine the purpose of the campaign. The principal object of the new concern may be to obtain distribution. The object of the old, well-established concern may be either to secure more dealer cooperation or to create more consumer demand. An advertising campaign without a purpose is like a ship without a destination.

4.The time required. Although an advertising campaign ordinarily is planned for a year, it should be extended over a sufficient length of time to enable the advertiser reasonably to expect the result desired. Too many advertisers become discouraged just when they arena the point of succeeding.

An advertising agent was asked once how long he thought it would be necessary to test the advantages of advertising for a particular product. Before answering he asked the advertiser, "How often does the same consumer buy your class of products?" He was told the consumer reordered every three to six months. He pointed out to the prospective client that if he advertised continuously for six months and secured all the business in his market, he would then just have a chance to catch each buyer on his next order. In other words, if each buyer were fully convinced by the advertising, six months would only allow each one an opportunity to purchase once. The advertising campaign was started on the six months' basis. At the end of four months the advertiser became discouraged. The agent reminded his client of his estimate, and asked the privilege of sending a letter to a selected list of the advertiser's prospects. With this letter the agent sent a return postal, on which one of the questions asked was, "How often do you order a product of this kind?" The return postals showed that, while the shortest time was three months, the longest was three years, and the average was eleven and one-quarter months. Other questions asked on the card were: "In what quantities do you order?" and "If you were ordering today, what brand would you specify?" The answers to these two questions indicated a volume of business that would have been equal to a 150 per cent increase in the advertiser's annual business if the buyers had been in a position to order at that time. Yet the advertiser was ready to admit that his advertising campaign was a failure. He had not given the advertising time to show results.

5. *Effect of the campaign on the advertiser.* When a manufacturer decides seriously to undertake a planned advertising campaign, he immediately changes from. the position of letting himself be sold advertising to the position of buying advertising. Undoubtedly the greatest waste in advertising today is indiscriminate purchasing of space and of materials. In many businesses those items of expense which cannot rightly be charged to production or distribution are charged to the advertising department. This department has to bear the burden, for example, of donations and charity which have no direct relation to advertising, but are charged to it because the advertising account is elastic. When one lays out an advertising campaign, he plans all expenditures, and nothing can creep in that does not

definitely bear on his purpose. A campaign is something tangible. The advertiser planning a campaign begins to weigh values. He begins to establish a policy. He sends his order for advertisements in certain media unsolicited, because, from the data he has before him, he feels that these media will bring him the greatest return on the money invested.

A certain manufacturer spent $40,000 a year in advertising without any definitely planned campaign. One of the items was $5,000 for flange signs. The reason he spent $5,000 was because the price in five thousand lots brought the sign down to one dollar each, while, if he had purchased in one thousand lots, the signs would have cost two dollars each. When the signs had been in the manufacturer's possession for over three years, his salesmen had not as yet been able to find five thousand dealers who would use them. Five hundred signs could have been purchased for $1,250, thus saving the manufacturer $3,750. Such examples of waste are often found among concerns having no definitely outlined advertising campaigns.

When a manufacturer outlines and attempts to conduct an advertising campaign, he knows exactly where and when he is spending his money. He keeps accurate record of the returns. He begins to have greater faith in advertising as the returns materialize. He begins to see bigger possibilities in his business. He learns to plan ahead. The concern which definitely lays out and carries forward an advertising campaign has made its first step toward advertising success. The day of profit in hit-or-miss advertising has gone. Without the campaign there is little chance for success.

6. *Effect of the campaign on salesmen*. The concern which buys its advertising space on the hit-or-miss basis, has no opportunity to inspire its sales force with a realization of what it is doing. Advertising makes it possible for salesmen to close sales quickly. Advertising gives salesmen confidence. A manufacturer who had been buying advertising by the hit-or-miss method determined on a definite campaign for the sale of one of his products, and at a convention at the beginning of the season outlined the campaign to his salesmen. After describing the campaign and the new merchandising plan behind the advertising, he asked each salesman to establish his own quota of sales which he expected to make during the year with the assistance of the advertising. To the manufacturer's surprise and pleasure, the quotas established by the salesmen themselves totaled a 500 per cent increase in his business on the article advertised. That the salesmen were not far wrong in

their estimate is indicated by the result at the end of the year, which showed an actual increase of 625 per cent. This example of the effect of the campaign on the salesmen is especially interesting when it is realized that the advertiser spent no more money in the campaign than he had spent the previous year under the hit-or-miss "buy what is presented" method.

7. *Effect of the campaign on dealers.* One of the first questions a dealer asks a salesman is, "What assurance will I have of consumer demand? Is the article going to be advertised and how?" The old reply, "Oh, my company is spending a large amount of money in advertising," is no longer convincing. Dealers, familiar with the powerful influence of advertising, wish to know the media used, the amount of space contracted for, and the quality of the advertisements themselves. Without a definite campaign laid out in advance, salesmen are unable to give dealers this information. And on this ground alone, dealers often refuse to stock the goods.

When the campaign is laid out in advance and dealers are told of the advertising, when and Where it will appear, they are in a position to take advantage of the advertising of the manufacturer to call the attention of the public to the fact that they distribute the article advertised. Many dealers are willing to spend their own money to connect their stores as distributing centers with national advertising. Advertisers often arrange special advertising "drives" for limited periods, keeping dealers informed of the dates of these special efforts in the campaign. During the "drives" increased space may be taken in the national magazines and also in the newspapers and in other media, in specific localities.

This unusual effort encourages dealers to mention the advertised article in their own newspaper advertisements and to trim their windows with the articles advertised. Advertisers are beginning to learn that they cannot expect much dealer cooperation without definite campaigns planned well in advance, and without giving notice to their dealers of their plans.

8. *Effect of the campaign on consumers.* The steady, persistent flow of the river wears away the rock. Advertising is powerful, but the power of advertising must be used as the suggestion of a friend, not as the command of a superior officer. Most of us cannot tell what particular influence first induced us to buy any of the advertised products we are now using. Many people use Ivory Soap as a matter of course. They cannot tell what advertisement persuaded them to use it or what advertisement persuaded their parents first to use it. They somehow feel, however,

that when they are using it they are using the popular soap, the pure soap, the soap which it is customary to use. The Procter and Gamble Company might stop advertising for a time, and many of us would still continue to use Ivory Soap. It would not be long, however, before the standing which Ivory Soap has in the minds of many people today would be forgotten. A new generation would spring up unfamiliar with the Ivory Soap advertising. Competitors would have been educating this generation to demand their soaps, and in time (in a shorter time than most of us realize) another soap would probably become the popular favorite.

Popularity of a product cannot be gained by spasmodic advertising. Back of the advertising there must be a plan; there must be a purpose—a unity of purpose. And there must be continuity. The public likes to purchase the popular article. The public likes to know why. The public likes to be constantly reminded. Constant repetition is a great aid to memory.

To the persistent advertiser the public gives that intangible yet supremely valuable asset known as good-will. The good-will of a business is like the character of an individual. Seemingly it may be as firm as the rock of Gibraltar, and yet it may be entirely destroyed in a day. James Pyle's Pearline was advertised persistently from 1877 to 1907. In 1904 the appropriation amounted to $500,000. In 1907, the last of the Pyle family had died and the business was being conducted by the representatives of two estates. It was felt that Pearline was sufficiently well known to allow the company to discontinue advertising for a few years. The experiment proved fatal. In 1914, the Procter and Gamble Company bought James Pyle's Pearline, thus saving the company, it is said, from actual bankruptcy.

9. *Effect of the campaign on the product.* When one is in the limelight, he must live up to the reputation created for him, or expect failure more quickly than if he remained in the shadow. Advertising creates popularity for worthy products only. Advertising will only accelerate the failure of an unworthy product. As soon as a manufacturer puts his name on his product, he feels an added personal responsibility for its quality. Trade-marking and advertising have, perhaps, done more to improve the quality of merchandise than any other influence, not excepting pure food laws and factory regulations. Mr. Myron McMillan of the J. T. McMillan Company, packers, recalls a case in point. When he first began to advertise Paragon Bacon, he chose streetcar cards as a medium so that he might be able to show slices of bacon in the actual colors. He employed a noted artist to paint a picture of his bacon. The proper proportion of fat and lean strips made everyone's mouth

water. The card had been in the street car but a few days, when, on talking with his superintendent, Mr. McMillan learned that his product did not look like the picture on the street-car card. The superintendent said: "Nobody cuts bacon that way." Mr. McMillan replied: "I advertised this bacon because I thought it was the finest bacon that could be made. Here I find in my own packing house a man who knew how to improve the quality and had not told me of it. The cards are in the street cars, and we must deliver the quality represented. I don't care what it costs; as long as we are advertising this bacon cut to waste, if necessary, but give us the cut represented in the pictures." The new cutting was so popular that it has never been changed to this day, and the J. T. McMillan Company finds the public is perfectly willing to pay the additional price which allows the packer to cut to waste in order to present the perfect slice.

When the product is once advertised, the wise manufacturer realizes that it must always be kept up to standard and that his success depends on keeping up the quality rather than on taking advantage of a reputation made thru advertising. Improvement in quality gives talking points for advertisements. There is no question that the automobile was brought to perfection more rapidly thru the yearly seeking of manufacturers for new talking points for their advertisements than it would have been if the automobile had not been advertised.

10. *The campaign as a great educator.* Advertising campaigns have educated the world to the use of the automobile. In twenty years persistent, carefully planned advertising has educated the nation to the use of porcelain bath tubs. Advertising campaigns have explained the uses of new inventions, have described new discoveries, have pictured new methods. In a story entitled: "A World Without Advertising," prepared for the Associated Advertising Clubs of the World, Mr. Forrest Crissey makes the following interesting prophecy: All these calamities involved in A World Without Advertising are small and scarcely to be considered when compared with the blow that would be dealt to education by such a holocaust of elimination. Aside from the common school system of the United States advertising is undoubtedly the greatest educational force in existence. Perhaps even this exception is debatable but advertising has no need to claim more than its own in any field and it can do and will gladly do for the common schools for formal education far more than it has ever been asked or permitted to do.

There is in man an impulse for larger living that is the very seed of progress. The individual, the community, the nation in which this impulse is undeveloped, faces certain stagnation. Nothing else stimulates this natural hunger for an expanding experience in every rightful direction as does advertising. Always it prompts man to move forward, to want more things, better things, finer things. It is the official advance agent of Invention, of Science, of Art and of Education.

11. *Advertising and selling expense.* In the Text on "Marketing and Merchandising" a chapter is devoted to the consideration of the effect of advertising on the selling price of the thing advertised. This is so important a subject, and one which so vitally concerns the future of advertising and the attitude of the public toward all publicity, that it is well here to give additional illustrations of the influence of advertising on prices and to review the arguments which definitely justify advertising as a legitimate, economical, and generally beneficial method of marketing.

The first thing an advertising campaign is expected to accomplish is volume of sales. In obtaining volume the advertiser usually finds that he also decreases his selling cost per unit. Suppose you and a certain competitor are each making annually a million boxes of your products. Assume that you each have been doing no advertising, but have sold thru salesmen alone, and your salesmen have cost you $100,000. This is a selling cost for each of you of ten cents a box. You each make a net profit of $50,000, or five cents a box.

Now suppose your competitor decides to put forth an extra effort to increase his volume and to popularize his brand by advertising. A salesman can take an order for ten dozens just as easily as he can for one-twelfth of a dozen if the demand has been created. One of the purposes of advertising is to create demand.

Suppose that next year, or the year after, your competitor appropriates $100,000 for advertising, making his total selling expense $200,000. But in doing this, the advertising so increases his volume of sales that he is able to dispose of 4,000,000 boxes. If it costs him $200,000 to sell 4,000,000 boxes, his selling cost is now five cents a box, while yours, without advertising is still ten cents. He not only makes four times the gross profit that you make, because he sells four times as much, but he makes another profit of five cents for every box sold, because he can sell a box at half what it cost you to sell one.

How will this affect you? You may not notice the effect while times are good and you and your competitor maintain the same price. But let a crisis come, or let your competitor see that he can increase his volume of business still further by lowering his price to the consumer, and he can practically put you out of business any time he wants to. He holds you in the hollow of his hand. You are beaten any time he says the word. Thru advertising he has cut his cost to a place where he can make a good profit and still sell at a price below your actual cost.

12. *Campaigns that cut manufacturers' costs.* When Hart, Schaffner & Marx began to advertise, the house was doing an annual business of $1,500,000. Ten years later this had increased to $15,000,000. An interesting comparison of selling costs and amounts spent for magazine advertising by four ready-to-wear clothing manufacturers was compiled by Printers' Ink about the time Hart, Schaffner & Marx reached the fifteen million mark. The selling costs include cost of salesmen only the percentages are based on total sales.

	Magazine Advertising	Selling Cost
Hart, Schaffner & Marx	$85,000	2 ½ to 3%
B. Kuppenheimer & Co	49,000	4%
Samuel W. Peck & Co	29,000	6%
Alfred Benjamin	24,000	7%

13. *Campaigns that have cut retailers costs.* Retailers are not slow to realize that this same power which cuts manufacturers' costs will also out their costs. By spending a sufficient amount in advertising they can so increase their volume of business that, while the gross profit of each item may be decreased, the net profit will increase. The following figures are taken from records of the actual experiences of one of the retail distributors of Hart, Schaffner & Marx clothing company.

	First Half 1918	Second Half 1918	1919
Percentage of advertising appropriation to sales of previous period	2.40%	6.35%	9.46%
Percentage of sales of current period to sales of previous period	63.78%	126.40%	197.80%
Percentage of advertising	3.77%	5.00%	4.78%

expenditure of current period to
sales of current period

Gross Profit	41.40%	38.60%	37.70%
Net Profit	4.81%	8.24%	11.02%

14. *Experience the best guide.* Advertising is a subject which is very much alive. It has few traditions, and only a slowly growing body of principles. Two advertising experts may recommend entirely different solutions of the same advertising problem, and both of the solutions may be right. Two campaigns, to accomplish the same thing, have often been conducted in entirely different ways, both proving successful. Because of this plastic state of the art of advertising—because the one best campaign for a given advertiser must still be partly a matter of opinion— it is impossible to lay down a set of hard and fast rules for the planning of advertising campaigns. And yet certain general principles have been developed from experience. The advertising world has begun compare experiences, and to find that in planning a campaign the advertiser or his agent usually asks himself certain fundamental questions which must be adequately answered before any campaign can properly launched. It is our purpose in the following chapters to outline some of these questions and to tell how the answers to them have affected the results of actual campaigns. We are to give the records of tangible results, rather than the opinions of individuals. The reader will be expected to draw his own conclusions as to how the basic questions should be answered in planning a campaign for the business in which he is most interested.

ADVISORY 2

ANALYSIS or DEMAND AND COMPETITION

1. *Preliminaries of the campaign.* Advertising is costly, and frequently considerable time must elapse before returns can reasonably be expected from the investment. The advertiser who would avoid expensive and ruinous mistakes should know definitely in advance just what he plans to accomplish and What obstacles are to be overcome in so doing. When advertising was regarded rather as a gamble than an investment there were few preliminary investigations before campaigns were launched. Even today advertising in the dark is not unknown. Stories are told of concerns which have conducted newspaper campaigns to sell electric toasters and electric flat irons, in cities not equipped with electric light and power.

The importance of investigation before the formulation of selling plans and policies has been clearly set forth in the Modern Business Text on "Marketing and Merchandising." The product must be carefully tested. Its selling points must be listed. Trade channels must be selected. Competition must be reckoned with. Problems of the trade-mark and package must be solved.

These are only a few of the matters to be considered in an exhaustive analysis that should be undertaken to determine the whole sales policy and the marketing campaign, whether thru salesmen or thru advertising or thru a combination of the two. Many of these matters have received attention in the earlier volumes of the Text. At this point the reader is asked to consider those which present special problems for the advertiser. Questions now to be considered group themselves chiefly about the analysis of possible demand and the analysis of competition.

2. *Developing demand.* In whatever manner the sales policy may associate personal salesmanship and advertising, the immediate object of the latter is to develop a demand for the advertised product. According to circumstances the problem of the advertiser may be (1) to create a demand for an article which is familiar to the public; (2) to extend the use of an article already known, or (3) to attract to the particular product advertised a part of the demand which already exists. Of course it must be understood that demand is not limited and is in most cases susceptible of expansion so that the second and third aspects of demand creation tend to merge into one another.

3. *Educational campaigns.* When the article is entirely new the advertiser must incur a large expense in what he terms educational effort. He must familiarize the buying public with the uses of the article and the service which it can render to the buyer. Most of us can recall when such articles as Dictaphones, Thermos bottles, cash registers and washing machines were distinct novelties. That they are no longer such is due in large part to persistent advertising.

Scarcely less will be the necessary outlay when the advertiser seeks to extend the use of a product by bringing what has been deemed a luxury into the category of necessities. Ten years ago automobile manufacturers featured the convenience of the automobile to the physician, who, by using it, could make his ordinary calls quickly, and its necessity in urgent calls in which a life was in danger and the old fashioned buggy too slow. They showed how the automobile enabled the business man to make more money in his business and get his family out in the open air. Such advertising effort has made the automobile a necessity to one-fifth of the families of the United States. The Curtiss Company and Glen Martin in advertising airplanes are now educating the public along the same line. Instead of talking about. the airplane as a luxury for touring travel or of emphasizing the mechanical difference between their planes they show the advantages of a plane to a businessman in Saving time and expense in traveling to keep most important engagements.

Thru such painstaking analysis of the possible demand advertisers not only build up business but lead the world to require the highest standards of living.

4. *Diverting demand.* If, on the other hand, the article is simply a new brand of a class of goods already on the market, the advertiser must focus his attention upon plans to attract to his own product patronage which has perhaps heretofore gone to competing brands. He must show why his product is superior in quality. He may emphasize its lower price, but he always seeks by persistent repetition to associate his particular brand with the species of articles to which it belongs. Many of us have to think twice to recall that there are corn flakes other than Kellogg's, or rubber heels other than O'Sullivan's. Again, the advertiser may, by putting his brand on the tip of everyone's tongue, induce people from idle curiosity to compare his much vaunted goods with other brands with which they are already satisfied. Nevertheless, the chief purpose of the advertiser in these cases is permanently to divert a demand already existing.

Of course, no business organization need subsist entirely upon diverted demand; the possibility of developing new demand always exists. Tho candles are an age-old product, a new candle industry might conceivably depend largely upon developed demand. In its advertising the new industry might contrast the fierce, glaring light of electric bulbs with the mellow, golden glow of the candle till in the end no hostess would regard her dinner table complete without its array of candles. Spaghetti, a household article for centuries, may thru energetic advertising assume as large a place on the American menu as that which it now occupies in Italy. Rice might be pushed to the place it occupies in oriental lands. A few years ago a number of toilet soap companies sought, by combining, to save the advertising expense which they believed had previously served merely to divert demand from one to another of the companies. When the companies curtailed their advertising, the demand for toilet soaps dwindled seriously.

5. *Demand and the repeat element.* In investigating the yearly demand for any product, it is important to consider how much time will elapse before a satisfied customer will come back for more. Is the product of such a nature that but one sale can be made to a customer during his lifetime, or will he buy once a year, once a month, or once each week? Is the product a fad or novelty?

Failing to study the demand in advance, one might get well under way in a campaign and then suddenly discover that every person in the territory who cared to buy had purchased and that further sales must wait for a new generation. Not infrequently it costs more than the selling price to gain the confidence of a customer. In most businesses the profit is in the reorder. The business which will have a new market of already convinced customers every six months may need a different advertising policy from the one that must wait a year for repeat orders. In utilizing this repeat element, great ingenuity has sometimes been employed. One method successfully used is that of a "family of products." The world was made familiar with Quaker Oats, and readily accepted Quaker Puffed Rice and Quaker Puffed Wheat. Every one knows the "57 Varieties," now increased to a yet greater number. After a reputation for one product has been established, it is easier to create a demand for another product under the same family name than to start with an entirely new name and make a reputation for it. The manufacturer of a group of products of common characteristics bound together by a common name can offset the lack of "repeat" in the individual members of his line by the demand he can create for other members.

In some cases the "family" is small and its members have quite a close resemblance one with another, While in other cases the family has grown so large that only the name appears to hold it together. Under such talismanic names as Armour's and Beechnut we find grouped products as diverse as lard and grape juice, bacon and chewing gum. None the less the advertising effort spent upon one member of the family accrues to the advantage of all that bear the name

It was felt that advertising without a record of success to feature would be unprofitable. The fact that National Cash Registers were not advertised at first may have been quite as much the result of such a policy as of the influence of convention in the days when advertising was less common.

Evidently there is a time as well as a place for advertising.

6. *Advertising with the season.* Time figures strategically in the development of demand for that immense class of goods subject more or less to seasons. For advertisers of goods of this class sold thru dealers, the dealers' season figures as prominently as the consumers' season. These seasons are identical for some products—automobiles, for example. For others, such as wearing apparel, six months or more may elapse between two seasons. Knowing this, the advertising man plans accordingly. His "dealer literature" and his "consumer literature" he prepares at the same time, with a view to showing the dealer reproductions of the consumer literature to follow. The salesmen in visiting the dealers use this to advantage. In some cases their whole selling talk wisely centers about what the manufacturer plans to do to develop consumer demand.

7. *Advertising against the season.* Manufactures and dealers are beginning to question whether in certain cases there is any real reason for a seasonal demand. They seek thru advertising to overcome slack seasons, using advertising in an attempt to do what electricians call "superimposing the peak upon the valley." That is, they are trying to raise the sale in the dull season, and lower it, if necessary, in the good season, to make a more even output the year round. Thru advertising California is selling walnuts in summer and lemons in winter, when before there was practically no sale for these products in these seasons. Advertising makes business grow in seasons that without it would be dull.

8. *Competition.* It is not enough for the manufacturer to study the possible demand for his product. He should know as accurately as possible what others, his competitors, are doing to satisfy that demand. Such knowledge if reliable and accurate is useful not only in advertising but, as explained in the Modern Business Text on "Marketing and Merchandising", in determining the entire sales policy.

Much that passes for information concerning what competitors are doing is mere gossip and practically worthless. It is difficult to obtain reliable information about one's competitors, but that should not deter one from spending time and money to secure definite information so far as possible concerning them. Of course if the purpose of seeking this information is blindly to copy others in advertising and other policies it is so much time and money wasted. Constructive business policies may be built upon research but not on imitation.

Too many manufacturers are prone to sweep aside the question of competition with the egotistical remark "We have no competitors." This no doubt would be important if true, but it is rarely true. If true, it does not follow that the advertising should be wholly of the constructive and educational type rather than purely competitive. But the remark is seldom true since the fact that another concern may make an article inferior in quality to yours, or one that is sold at a different price, is no proof that it does not compete with yours on the market. The wise advertiser will study his competing products and their selling points just as carefully as he does his own.

9. *Comparison of good-will.* One should ascertain as nearly as possible the amount of advertising which each competitor has done and the amount of good-will which

each has obtained thru his advertising and thru the satisfaction which his products have given.

A manufacturer whose plant is estimated to be worth about two million dollars recently remarked: "If I were forced to choose between sacrificing my plant and the good-will which this company has established thru continuous advertising for the last twenty years, I should willingly say, 'Burn down the plant. I can obtain capital to rebuild it tomorrow, because our advertising has created a demand which has a bankable value and will bring new capital.' This is our strongest bulwark against competition. A new plant can be built in ninety days. But our advertising has taken years, and no amount of capital could substitute for the impression it has made." It is important, therefore, that the advertiser determine how long each competitor has been established and how long each has been advertising continuously.

Merely a list of the advertising schedules of one's competitors, however, will not necessarily provide a basis for an estimate of the good-will each enjoys. One should learn of the friendships which competitors have established with the trade and with consumers, together with the methods employed to obtain these friendships. Only in this way can the new advertiser intelligently lay plans for the building up of good-will for his own name and for his own products.

10. *Comparison of advertising.* It is well to have a scrap-book and to keep in it copies of the advertisements of competitors. There is no particular advantage in referring to it daily but, at the end of the year, by comparing it with the records of your own sales and those of your competitors you will have a basis for judging the value of competing advertising which is far better than mere opinion or hearsay. In planning a campaign it is always advisable to list the publications in which each competitor has advertised and to find out how much each publication has been used. In active competition a manufacturer always tries to reach the same buyers that his competitors are reaching. Do not jump at the conclusion, however, that just because a competitor is using certain publications his investment is proving profitable. An advertising agency recently planned a national campaign for a manufacturer who at first insisted on using every medium his principal competitor was using. The agent found that in many publications the competitor had contracts for but one insertion, and, from the nature of the product and the medium, the agent was certain the competitor lost money. On more thorough investigation, the agent found that the competitor was simply a plunger

and that he had no plans or records to guide him in his advertising. He found, however, that another, a much younger and smaller competitor, kept very careful records of returns. The advertising schedule of the small competitor proved to be a much better guide for the new advertiser than the list of media used by the larger and more important manufacturer.

A large western paint house recently decided to advertise in farm journals. It wanted to dominate the field. Fourteen competitors had been using farm journals for many years. The paint manufacturer asked his advertising agent to obtain for him schedules of the advertising of all his competitors for the five years previous. These schedules showed that all the competitors began to advertise in the first weeks of February. So he ordered his advertising to commence the middle of January. He also made his advertisements a little larger in size than those of any of his competitors. By making a careful investigation and by doing the things to which a study of competing advertising logically pointed, he was able to dominate his field from the beginning.

11. *Studying at competitor's follow-up.* A common method of keeping track of competitive advertising consists simply in responding to a competitor's advertising and in keeping accurate record of the way in which the competitor answers and follows up the inquiry. The inquiry is usually made in the name of some one who might be considered a possible purchaser. As each letter or piece of literature comes in; it is dated and compared for appearance, quality, and the impression it creates with other literature received from other competitors. By this method an advertiser is able to learn the following facts in relation to competition:

a. How promptly inquiries are answered.
b. How many pieces of literature are sent to each prospect.
c. The quality of letters used—whether all inquiries are answered with personal letters, multigraphed letters or printed literature.
d. The cost of a competitor's follow-up. This can be roughly estimated by adding the cost of postage to the probable cost of the letters and the other advertising literature that is received.
e. The relative emphasis given to each sales argument. This is an interesting test. A complete set of each competitor's literature is taken and the sales arguments of each listed. Then a record is made of the proportion of space used for each argument and the order in which the arguments are introduced. Such a test often reveals some most valuable facts.

f. How completely the sales organization cooperates with the advertising department.

12. *Correcting errors by studying competitors.* A manufacturer of trucks wanted to know the sales and advertising methods used by his competitors. He found that while he was using form letters to answer inquiries, twelve of his fourteen competitors were using personal letters and referring in these letters to trucks they had sold to buyers located in the city or district from which the inquiry came. This led to his keeping an accurate record and a set of testimonial letters for every truck he sold. He found that eight of the fourteen competitors spent a dollar and a half on each inquirer in letters and booklets. The most striking discovery was made in studying the dates on which the different pieces of literature were received and the promptness with which the district representatives of his competitors called on the inquirer. Twelve of the fourteen competitors sent a sales representative to call on the inquirer before he received or could have received a letter from the manufacturer in reply to his inquiry. This clearly indicated that these twelve manufacturers did not wait for the mails, but were in the habit of wiring their district agents on receipt of inquiries from responsible persons. The manufacturer who conducted the investigation had not been doing this. He had been losing considerable business in his own territory, but until he made this analysis he could not understand why.

13. *Comparison of sales policies.* Advertising; the putting of one's sales arguments on paper, has probably had more to do with developing sales policies and the ideals of business than any other force. A non-advertiser usually follows the crowd. But as soon as advertising is undertaken, definite sales policies must be chosen and adhered to. Many advertising campaigns have had for their purposes the remedying of some particular sales conditions. One manufacturer has a competitor who is in the habit of overselling. It might seem that to avoid substitution by dealers, the only way to meet such competition would be to oversell also. But the sales manager, realizing the weapon he would have by pursuing a different policy, instructs his men to undersell rather than oversell, and to make a talking point of it. The advertising man, seeing his advantage, calls the attention of the public to the fact that his goods in the dealers' hands are always fresh; and the policy of competitors is thus made to pay handsome returns.

14. *Comparison of freight advantages.* In the distribution of many commodities, such as building materials and household furniture, some competitors have great

advantages over others in freight rates. In determining on advertising campaigns to reach new territories, it is desirable to compare freight rates in these cases and to choose for extensive advertising those territories in which one has at least equal shipping opportunities with competitors. A map showing the location of each competitor and the territory into which he can economically ship, is helpful in choosing advertising mediums. Such a map should be compared with the circulation records of each advertising medium in each territory that is considered.

15. *Relative importance of competitors*. In planning an advertising campaign one should decide whether he is in a position to dominate his field, so far as the force of advertising is concerned, or whether it would be better for him to use smaller space, perhaps more frequently, relying for the supreme competitive efforts on the sales force.

The A Company manufactures a specialty for farmers. It finds that 75 per cent of the business in its line is now done by one competitor. The remaining 25 per cent is divided among fifteen other small concerns of which the A Company is one. The leading competitor has used educational copy and large space in agricultural publications for five years. The business of the A Company will not warrant competition with the leader either in size of appropriation or in amount of space used. The A Company's advertising manager decides under these conditions to take smaller space but to appear in the agricultural publications regularly, always appearing in each issue in which his chief competitor appears. The copy is intended to bring inquiries at low expense, rather than to make sales, on the theory that a farmer will wish to investigate more than one make of the particular specialty before he buys, and that if each advertiser receives an inquiry or a proportion of the inquiries, he must leave the closing of the sale to his sales force.

An entirely different plan of procedure was adopted by a maker of men's furnishings. On investigation he found that while one competitor stood out head and shoulders above all others, this competitor actually controlled only 25 per cent of the market; the investigator controlled 12 per cent; another competitor controlled 10 per cent; and the rest of the market was divided among 30 competitors controlling in no case more than 7 per cent each. The leader in the field, while spending a certain amount for advertising, did not spend in proportion to the amount of business controlled. The manufacturer in question decided that there was an opportunity for him to become the leader in his line. While he was not the leader in volume of sales, he determined that his advertising should have the appearance of leadership. He employed a famous illustrator to make all the illustrations for his advertisements. All the type was hand-lettered by the best designers. His cuts were in every way superior to those of his competitors. The size of space used was carefully planned to be larger and more commanding than that of his competitors. This plan was consistently followed throughout all the advertising, and today this manufacturer controls over 70 per cent of the business on his line.

ADVISORY 3

THE ADVERTISING APPROPRIATION

1. *How much to spend for advertising.* The answer to the question, "How much will it cost to advertise?" is much like the answer to the question, "How much will it cost to build a house?" A house may cost all the way from a few hundred dollars to a few million dollars, depending on what the owner needs or thinks he needs. If it is only shelter he; wants he may obtain it very cheaply, but mere shelter is not the only consideration. Before a man starts to build a house, he usually has in mind an approximate price which he hopes will build for him a house representative of his social standing. Even in the same social group, two men may spend widely varying amounts for their homes, depending on their tastes and the size of their families. In advertising, the amount of the investment depends on the purpose to be achieved, on the actual or desired position of the advertiser in his field, and on his individual tastes and preferences.

2. *The value of records.* Some mail-order advertisers have kept records for years, so they feel they can tell within a few hundred dollars the amount of business that may be secured from any given appropriation. In this chapter we shall discuss the different methods employed by leading advertisers in determining their annual advertising appropriations, and shall leave the reader to choose what he considers the best method to follow in planning an advertising campaign for any product that he might wish to advertise.

3. *Time required to reduce selling cost per unit.* Advertising requires three things: time, money and intelligence. At the start of a campaign, advertising seldom pays; it usually takes time to produce satisfactory results. As the farmer plants his seed and waits, knowing full well that, if the seed is right and the soil is right, the

harvest will come; so the advertiser invests his money and waits, knowing full well that, if his advertisements are intelligently prepared and if he has chosen his market and his plan carefully, time will bring the harvest.

When the Russell-Miller Milling Company began to advertise Occident Flour, the officers knew that successful advertising does three things: First, it increases the asset of good-will in a business.

Second, it produces volume of sales, which usually results in decreased manufacturing cost per unit.

Third, by increasing the volume it ultimately decreases the unit selling cost. As none of these things comes in a-minute or a month, the advertising expense was neither immediately listed as an asset nor charged to selling expense. The first appropriation was for $600,000, one-third of this to be spent annually for three consecutive years.

"Our expenditure for advertising," said Mr. H, S. Helm, the general manager, "was undertaken with no thought or expectation of an early harvest on the seed sown. It was considered at the start that material returns should not be conservatively looked for short of three years' continuous advertising.

"The undertaking was looked upon and treated as an investment in good-will and insurance on business already established. It was perfectly plain that the current business, or that of the very near future, could not stand an increase in per barrel selling cost to absorb the advertising expense. We therefore made our appropriation covering a period of three years and prepared to charge the advertising out as expended from past earnings and surplus until such time as it could be charged to the current selling cost without increasing the per barrel selling cost."

Six hundred thousand dollars, on an intangible and new venture, taken right out of past profits, requires nerve, as every advertising man knows; but the results have already proved the soundness of the theory; the selling cost per barrel so decreased that instead of waiting three years, after the end of the second year the company charged the advertising expense as part of the current selling expense. And still the investment in good-will, because it is real good-will, goes on drawing compound interest. During the first two years of national advertising, the increase in sales was more than five times the increase in selling expense.

4. *When advertising begins to bear fruit.* An interesting example of the way advertising affects the sales curve is shown in the accompanying illustration, taken from the records of the business of the Way Sagless Spring Company. From the beginning of 1910 to the middle of 1912 the advertising appropriation in dollars greatly exceeded the sales of springs. After the middle of 1912, while the advertising appropriation constantly increased, the sales curve increased at a much faster rate. Since 1916 sales in Springs have not increased in the saint ratio as sales in dollars. The drop in advertising in 1918 is reflected in sales though it was in part due to the difficulty in securing raw material. Experiences such as this lead advertising men to believe that in the beginning the amount of the appropriation cannot be expected to have a direct ratio to the resulting sales.

5. **Basing the appropriation on a specified amount per unit of expected sales.** In attempting to insure permanent sales success some advertisers base their appropriations on a certain number of cents per unit of expected sales. They reason rightly that it is not enough to sell to jobbers and retailers alone. They must help the dealers to make sales to consumers. It is worth a certain amount per unit to assure the dealers that consumers will know of the product and will demand it.

The Dayton Engineering Laboratories Company sold 12,000 "Delco" starters to manufacturers in 1912. At the beginning of 1913, this company had already contracted with manufacturers for 25,000 systems. It decided that it could afford from sales expense a dollar for each system sold to educate the public to the merits of the starter. Therefore the first advertising appropriation was $25,000. The advertising was so successful, however, that the company actually sold 37,000 systems during 1913. The advertising appropriation has been increased each year on the basis of the number of systems contracted for, but the price of the system and the appropriation per unit have decreased, so that today the advertising appropriation is probably less than fifty cents a machine.

The Creamette Company plans to spend ten cents a case in advertising Creamettes. Each year the advertising appropriation is based on an amount equal to ten cents a case of expected sales. By following the sales curve the company is able to estimate approximately the number of cases it should sell during the year.

6. *Basing the appropriation on a certain amount per possible purchaser.* Other advertisers look at the problem from the angle of possible purchasers rather than sales. They consider advertising purely as memory insurance. Except in cases of very seasonable articles, one can never tell just when his prospects are thinking of buying. If an advertiser feels certain that his possible customers will remember his brand favorably whenever they are ready to buy, he may feel that his sales are more than half made. These advertisers consider it worth so much per buyer per year to be sure that their products will remain in the memories of their possible customers.

Coca-Cola, with its annual advertising appropriation, which is said to be more than $1,000,000, spends in this country of 106,000,000 people approximately a cent a year a prospect for memory insurance. A manufacturer of ornamental iron and bronze, which is used only in large buildings, spends two dollars a year a prospect for such insurance. There are in this country only 1,000 architects with whom he can do business profitably. His advertising costs $2,000 a year. Most of it is spent in reaching architects direct by mail. Coca-Cola, on the other hand, may be purchased by anyone, and everyone is a possible customer. When Coca-Cola makes a sale, the exchange is for a nickel. When the other man makes a sale, the sum involved runs into the hundreds of thousands of dollars. One can afford to pay more per unit. The other can afford to pay more in the total.

Ivory Soap is another example of a product with a practically universal appeal on which is spent approximately a penny a possible purchaser a year. Wm. Wrigley, Jr. is said to spend two cents a person a year to advertise his gums. His advertising appropriation is reported to amount to $2,500,000 annually.

7. *Basing the appropriation on the amount of capital available.* The average advertiser is not, however, in the financial position of the Coca-Cola Company, the Procter & Gamble Company, or William Wrigley, Jr. The question with him usually is, "How much can I afford?" In such cases the advertising campaign must be planned to fit the conditions. Even the largest national advertisers commenced in a small way. They planned their advertising campaigns to cover one city or one district; then, as their business grew, they extended the advertising until they finally secured national distribution and were able to make their appropriations on the basis of national demand.

In studying the different methods of determining the appropriation, one must bear this fact clearly in mind: It is just as unprofitable to spend too much as it is to spend too little; and the more quickly an advertiser can get his business into a condition in which it is possible to fix his advertising appropriation on some carefully selected and tested basis, the more certain will be his success.

8. *Basing the appropriation on cost per inquiry and per sale.* Probably the most scientific method of determining the appropriation is that adapted by a certain mail-order specialty house. They know exactly how much they can afford to spend to make a sale. After years of careful record keeping. they know what proportion of inquiries can be turned into sales and the cost of the follow-up literature for each inquiry. These advertisers usually place contracts for only a few advertisements in a publication at a time, carefully checking the cost per inquiry, and discontinuing the advertising whenever the cost per inquiry proves excessive.

A certain mail order advertiser can afford to pay $50 for his average sale and still make a reasonable profit on each sale. Each year he estimates the amount of investment his capital will allow him to make on this basis and the amount of business he can handle. He instructs his advertising agent to place advertising on this basis. His records show that he turns 5% of his inquiries into sales. Whenever the inquiry cost is more than $2.50, a publication is cut off the list and whenever the inquiry cost is less than that amount more space is used in that publication. Each week the advertiser furnishes the agency with a report of his inquiries and sales to date. The agent adds or cancels publications, increases or decreases space and changes plan of appeal as these accurate records of returns indicate. In some publications the advertiser can only afford to use one column, four inch space while in others he uses pages and in one publication he uses as many as four pages in each issue. Most mail order advertisers know what it has cost them per sale during a period of years and with these records they buy the increase in business which their available capital and conditions justify.

9. *Basing the appropriation on a proportion of the profits of the previous year.* An increase in the advertising appropriation is one of the most definite indications of a desire to grow. Some advertisers at the end of the year, instead of putting the profits of the business into surplus, put a certain amount into advertising for the coming year. One advertiser reasons that, as his business increases, he will need new plants and additions to his present factories. Each year he lays aside a

certain amount of his profits toward the day when he will need these new factories.

He also realizes that to obtain demand sufficient to require new factories, he must increase his advertising. He decides that if his profit amounts to twenty per cent, he will put five per cent of that profit into advertising and five per cent into surplus. If his profit amounts to thirty per cent, he will put ten per cent into advertising and ten per cent into surplus.

Many of our most successful advertisers have built their fortunes on the principle of putting all of their profits back into advertising during the period of their early growth. John Wanamaker started in business for himself April 8, 1861. At the close of the first day the cash drawer revealed a total intake of $24.67. Of this amount $24.00 was spent for advertising and 67 cents saved for making change next morning. Wanamaker followed that general policy for many years. Wm. Wrigley, who built up a business which now is said to amount to something in the neighborhood of $50,000,000 a year, started with an original capital of $32.00. For years he put all of his profits back into advertising. Twice he attempted to enter the New York market and failed. The first time he spent $100,000 for advertising. He went back and waited until he had another profit of $100,000 and tried it again. This attempt was also a failure. He then waited until he had $200,000 saved and as soon as he had it, he proceeded to New York and dropped it in the same place. This time his efforts met with success.

10. *Basing the appropriation on amount spent the previous year.* Many advertisers have no more definite basis for estimating their appropriations than the amount they spent the year previous. If this amount is used simply as a starting point from which to figure a possibly increased appropriation, there is no objection to its use. But if the advertiser blindly appropriates for one year the same amount he spent the year before, without regard to the developing needs of his business, he can hardly expect to meet changing conditions or to make progress. One of the leading advertising agents will not take an advertising account unless the advertiser is willing to increase his appropriation at least fifteen per cent each year. He does not care to handle an account unless the business of the advertiser is to grow, and he estimates fifteen per cent as the lowest normal, healthy increase of a business that does consistent advertising.

11. *Basing the appropriation on the space desired.* To make the desired impression with certain advertising campaigns, it is advisable to use a certain amount of space or else not to attempt advertising at all. If an advertiser wishes to dominate and to use only full pages, it will cost him a certain amount of money.

The magazine publicity of the National Cash Register Company is estimated on such a basis. An advertising campaign, using full pages, extending them a year, and carrying a definite message, could not possibly accomplish its purpose if the advertiser confined himself to small space—one column, three-inch copy; for instance. Such small space advertising would, in fact, make the opposite impression from that desired; it would be much better not to advertise at all than to spend so small an amount of money. Advertising men often have in mind a certain amount which it is necessary to spend in a national campaign for a product of general consumption, to accomplish satisfactory results. In planning such a campaign, one must first decide on the advertising needed and then estimate its cost.

12. *Basing the appropriation on a certain per cent of gross sales.* Probably the most popular plan of estimating the appropriation is on the basis of a certain per cent of gross sales. Some advertisers estimate on the basis of the sales of the previous year and others estimate on the basis of expected sales. This percentage differs, of course, for each class of business, usually for each business house in its class. Many advertising men object to this method because they contend that it costs a larger proportionate amount to build a business up than it does to keep it going. Up to a certain point, it also costs less proportionately to keep a big business going than it does to keep a small business going.

The advantages of the plan rest on the fact that a percentage basis gives every advertiser something definite to work on. From year to year an increasing number of business houses are beginning to know accurately their costs of doing business and are apportioning a definite proportion of this cost to each department. The Sherwin-Williams Company of Cleveland bases its advertising appropriation on three and a half per cent of its gross sales of all kinds of paint and other materials which it distributes. The Sherwin-Williams Company may put all of its advertising efforts on only one or two kinds of paint, but its appropriation is, nevertheless, based on its gross sales of all its products for the year. When asked why this method was adopted and how the three and a half per cent was arrived at, the advertising mam ager said, "We have found that our advertising should be this proportion of our cost of doing business. We find that we cannot make enough progress if we spend less, and that we cannot show enough profit if We spend more."

13. *Retailers' appropriations*. Retailers, dependent for the success of their advertising on sales made from day to day, and spending the larger amount of their appropriations in newspapers which are usually read and destroyed every twenty-four hours, are able to gauge the returns from their advertising more definitely than national advertisers. The prevailing custom among retailers is to base the appropriation on a certain percentage of gross sales. The retailer's cost of doing business is increasing, and the intelligent dealer knows exactly how much of this cost he can afford to appropriate for rent, how much for bad debts, how much for clerks and how much for advertising.

It is said that in the early days John Wranamaker was able to keep his advertising appropriation down close to two and one-half per cent of sales. Today his appropriation is said to reach five per cent. when Gimbel Brothers started their New York store they felt called upon to do aggressive advertising in anticipation of business, and are said to have spent considerably over six per cent. Leading authorities say that the successful department store of today should spend at least three per cent.

14. *Determining the proper percentage*. The ability to determine the proper percentage on greatest sales which any concern should spend for advertising is one of the greatest assets for success. Hart, Schaffner & Marx estimate that the retail clothier's normal proportion should be 5% of the season's sales. In evidence of this they cite the experience of a retailer in increasing and then decreasing his proportion below and above this percentage. The results of this experience were set forth by Mr. Joseph H. Schaffner in a pamphlet in which the facts were displayed in an interesting series of charts. Not less significant than the charts themselves were Mr. Schaffner's pertinent comments upon them. We may briefly review this experience.

2nd Season
Advertising appropriation 3.42 per cent of business of preceding year. Result, loss of 12.5 per cent in volume of business. Advertising cost became 3. 9 per cent of year's business.

This is Mr. Schaffner's comment:
"They planned to 'save' money and only spent an amount equal to 3.42% for advertising. By so doing they lost so much business that an advertising appropriation of 3.42% of last season's sales is now equal to an advertising expense of 3.9% of this season's business.

3rd Season
Advertising appropriation 4.68 per cent of business of preceding year. Result, 74 per cent increase in business over previous season. Advertising cost became 3.9 per cent of year's business.

Mr. Schaffner says:
"They appropriated 4.68% of 2nd season's sales for 3rd season's advertising. And business increased so rapidly that advertising turned out to be only 3.9% instead of 4.68% of current season's business."

4th Season
Advertising appropriation 2.4 per cent of business of preceding year. Result, loss of 36.22 per cent of last season's business. Advertising cost became 3.77 per cent of year's business.

Mr. Schaffner says:
"They evidently thought the business was growing so fast they didn't need to bother about advertising. Only appropriated 2.4% of the previous season's business and 'saved' the rest. And they lost so much business that advertising appropriation turned out to be 3.77% of current season, as against 2.4% of last."

5th Season
Advertising appropriation, 6.35 per cent of business of preceding year. Result, 26.4 per cent increase in business over previous season. Advertising cost only 5 per cent of year's business.

Mr. Schaffner's comment is as follows:
"They learned their lesson. This season they appropriated 6.35% for advertising. And their business increased to such an extent that their advertising appropriation turned out to be only 5% of their current season's sales after all."

1919 Business
Advertising appropriation 9.46 per cent of business of preceding year. Result, 97.8 per cent increase in business over previous season. Advertising cost 41.78 per cent of year's business.

Mr. Schaffner says: "It's easy to see they feel they've discovered the secret of success. It took a long test to convince them, but now they've gone in hook, line and sinker and appropriated 9.46% of their past year's sales for advertising. And they've rediscovered that old truth, that you really can't spend any money for advertising. The increased sales roll in so much faster than one can spend the money on advertising that even by appropriating 9.46% they couldn't get the percentage of advertising expenditure above 5%. The business increased so rapidly that of 9.46% last season's sales only amounted to 4.78% of the current season's."

These figures show very clearly the expensive advertising appropriations are of those which are too small and they demonstrate the soundness of judgment exhibited by such men as Wanamaker and

Wrigley that advertising is the force that brings returns in due proportion to the faith that the experienced advertiser places in it.

15. *Apportioning the appropriation*. The national advertiser in apportioning his appropriation has a much more difficult problem than that of the retailer. The question has often been asked, "How much should be apportioned to general publicity and how much to dealer advertising?" The amounts apportioned vary, from the Cream of Wheat Company, which spends one hundred per cent in general publicity, to Sears, Roebuck & Company, which spends practically all of its appropriation direct thru the mails. The advertising department of the Cream of Wheat Company, which is said to spend over $500,000 annually, consists of one man, Colonel Emery Mapes himself. The advertising department of Sears, Roebuck & Company consists of about 1500 people. No general rules can be given in regard to the division of appropriations, but the following figures may be of interest:

APPORTIONMENT OF PUBLICITY AND DEALER ADVERTISING IN DIFFERENT LINES

Classes of Merchandise	General Publicity	Dealer Publicity
4 Jewelry Manufacturers	73 per cent	27 per cent
4 Automobile Manufacturers	90 per cent	10 per cent
6 Food Manufacturers	85 per cent	15 per cent
3 Woman's Clothing Manufacturers	95 per cent	5 per cent
7 Office Equipment Manufacturers	75 per cent	25 per cent

ADVISORY 4

THE ADVERTISING AGENCY

1. ***What an advertising agency is.*** In the broadest use of the term, an advertising agency is an organization of merchandising and advertising experts who assist business houses in planning and carrying out advertising and sales campaigns. The advertising agent is a professional man. He resembles a physician in that his training and experience enable him to diagnose business troubles and to prescribe remedial measures. He resembles a lawyer in that he outlines a plan of campaign for his client and then pleads his client's case before the court of the people. His organization is a store-house of information regarding the pulling power of different advertising media, different copy, and different merchandising methods; he is expected to have all advertising principles and practices at his finger tips, and, after careful study, to be able to prescribe for any set of conditions the marketing methods that will bring the best results. The American Association of Advertising Agencies has given the following definition of agency service:

"Agency Service consists of interpreting to the public, or to that part of it which it is desired to reach, the advantages of a product or service. Interpreting to the public the advantages of a product or service is based upon:

1. A study of the product or service in order to determine the advantages and disadvantages. inherent in the product itself, and in its relation to competition.

2. An analysis of the present and potential market for which the product or service is adapted:
   - As to location
   - As to the extent of possible sale

- As to season
- As to trade and economic conditions
- As to nature and amount of competition.

3. A knowledge of the factors of distribution and sales and their methods of operation.

4. A knowledge of all the available media and means which can profitably be used to carry the interpretation of the product or service to consumer, wholesaler, dealer, contractor, or other factor. This knowledge covers:

- Character
- Influence || Quantity
- Circulation || Quality
- Physical Requirements || Location
- Costs

Acting on the study, analysis and knowledge as explained in the preceding paragraphs, recommendations are made and the following procedure ensues:

5. Formulation of a definite plan.

6. Execution of this plan:
   a. Writing, designing, illustrating of advertisements, or other appropriate forms of the message.
   b. Contracting for the space or other means of advertising.
   c. The proper incorporation of the message in mechanical form and forwarding it with proper instructions for the fulfilment of the contract.
   d. Checking and verifying of insertions, display or other means used.
   e. The auditing, billing and paying for the service, space and preparation.

7. Cooperation with the sales work, to insure the greatest effect from advertising.

2. *What an advertising agency does.* Advertising agencies differ greatly in their activities. Some do many things; some do only a few. Some concern themselves with all phases of a client's marketing problems; others confine their efforts to advertising alone. An agency that is completely organized to give advice regarding all phases of the distribution of a client's products and to handle as many details of

his entire sales campaign as he may wish to leave to the agency, ordinarily is equipped to do the following things:

First, the agency makes a careful study of the thing to be sold—its quality, as determined both by technical and by practical tests, the conditions under which it is manufactured, the sources of raw material, plant capacity, labor supply and costs of production; the capital of the business and the amount that can properly be invested in selling activity; the trade name and the trade-mark, with suggestions for changes if changes are desirable; the package, with particular reference to advertising value and to convenience in handling; and the selling points. It then makes an equally careful study of the market and the nature of the demand, finding out who the people are toward whom the sales effort should be directed, where they live, how they live, when they buy, how they buy, how much they will buy and from whom they buy, with an intensive investigation of competition in all its phases.

Next the agency studies the sales channels used by its client or that might be used by him, basing its recommendations on complete knowledge of the relations among manufacturers, jobbers, retailers and other middlemen, and determining for each particular product the best channels of trade from manufacturer to consumer. Following this the agency turns its attention to the price at which the product is to be sold and the sales policies to be followed—including such problems as credit, discounts, price maintenance, guarantees and service. After all this preliminary investigation and study, the completely equipped agency will, if the client wishes, aid in the organization or reorganization of the sales force, giving advice and active help in all the many problems of sales management. Coincident with this, the agency studies the copy problems of the advertiser, and writes, or assists in writing, the advertisements, obtains illustrations for them, attends to having the finished advertisements electrotyped, Selects the media to be used, sends the copy or the electrotyped plates to the periodicals selected, makes arrangements for all out-door and street-car advertising and checks the advertisements as they appear. Then come the important problems of coordinating the advertising with the work of the salesmen, or getting distribution among dealers and inducing them to cooperate in the campaign. This last problem involves the preparation of all sorts of dealer helps-x store signs, window displays, circulars, novelties, etc. The agency will also prepare direct advertising both to dealers and consumers, in the form of catalogs, house organs, sales letters, mailing cards and other kinds of direct sales helps. Finally, the agency either keeps careful records of the results of all the sales producing activity, or it advises and helps the client in keeping such records.

3. *History of the advertising agency.* The first advertising agency was established in 1840 in Philadelphia, by V. B. Palmer. In 1899, there were forty-one advertising agents. Today there are approximately 300 "recognized" agencies, while there are probably 150 other concerns attempting to conduct an agency business, but not receiving what is called "recognition" from any publishers' association. In addition, there are probably a thousand other individuals and organizations, who in limited fields of merchandising, copy and art assist advertisers with their campaigns.

In the beginning, the business of the advertising agent was very simple. He obtained permission to represent a list of newspapers, and called on prospective advertisers persuading them to "place their card" in a number of these newspapers. In those days, the papers for the most part had no established rates; the agent would make a rate to suit himself, paying the publisher as small a proportion of the amount collected as he could persuade him to take.

If the advertiser neglected to pay the agent, the agent was not held responsible for the space used.

In the early days, the basis of charge for advertising space was the "square." The publisher would divide a column into so many squares in which would be placed advertising "cards." The copy was seldom changed. In fact, some advertisements were used without change for from twenty to thirty years. The reader may recall "squares" used for long terms of years without substantial change of copy by Royal Baking Powder and Lea & Perrins Worcestershire Sauce.

In 1865, George P. Rowell established himself as an advertising agent, and it was he who introduced the plan of buying from the publishers a column or more of space in a list of 100 newspapers, dividing this into inch squares, taking full responsibility for payment, and on his own terms selling the inch squares to advertisers on annual contract. Some of this retailing of space was continued up to as late as the beginning of the twentieth century. A few people still believe that an agency is a dealer and has on hand contracts for space which he must use within a specified time and which he is, therefore, willing to sell at reduced rates. Advertising agents no longer operate in this way. The modern agency represents no particular media. It represents primarily its clients' interest, and places advertisements only in those media that can do the most to aid in the sale of its clients' goods.

While the advertising agent has guaranteed payment for the space used by his clients ever since the time of the Civil War, and has written copy and placed advertising from the beginning, it was not until about 1900 that agencies established their own art departments and began to render the general merchandising service that many of them render today.

4. *Publishers' representatives.* The early agent, of whom Mr. Rowell was a type, in buying space in selected papers and selling only that space, exercised a function of the modern "publisher's representative." A publisher's representative is the appointed representative of one or more publishers. It is his duty, in a certain territory, to call on advertising agents and on advertisers, presenting the merits of the publications he represents, and endeavoring to induce agents and their clients to place their advertisements in those publications.

5. *Agency's service to publisher.* Although the publishers of some classes of periodicals do not "recognize" advertising agencies, most publishers welcome the services of the agent and are glad to have him act as a valuable middleman between themselves and their advertisers. One reason for this is that publishers cannot keep as closely in touch with their advertisers as the agency can; also, it is much easier for a publisher to handle the accounts of a few agents than it would be to carry the accounts of many individual advertisers. One publisher finds that ninety per cent of the accounts he receives from the agencies repaid promptly every month, while only forty-eight per cent of the accounts he receives direct from advertisers are paid in this way.

The agency frequently saves the publisher from loss. As the agent's success depends on the success of his clients, he keeps advertisements out of publications where they would be likely to be unproductive. This keeps down the publishers' advertising death rate. So highly do most publications regard the services of the agent that, when a publisher is approached by a new advertiser who is not represented by an agent, the publisher will frequently send him to one for expert service for much the same reason that a court appoints an attorney for a defendant who has no legal representative to plead for him.

The chief service of the advertising agent to the publisher, however, is his ability to create business. The good advertising agency is one of the real constructive forces in American business. The agent is always on the lookout for new inventions and for new organizations with possibilities of growth. He must, of necessity, be optimistic; he must have vision. He continually preaches advertising and its possibilities. He studies it in all its forms; he believes in it and he impresses his belief upon others. Certainly a large proportion of the advertising carried by magazines and newspapers would never appear were it not for the work of the agent in seeking out possible advertisers, studying their business, smoothing out difficulties, "selling" the idea of advertising to the hesitating manufacturer, and finally carrying the great burden of the actual details of the advertising campaign.

6. *Agency's service to advertisers*. The advertising agent, as has already been demonstrated, is in a position to do many things for an advertiser. Agents speak of "developing" an account. For example, an advertising agent will sometimes render service and advice for a year or two before any advertising is placed. He may find many things in the organization needing correction before proper advantage may be taken of the advertising. Perhaps the advertiser's package is not sufficiently distinctive. Perhaps his plan of selling is not adaptable to larger fields. Whatever it is in the organization that is an obstacle to its large success, the province of the advertising agent is to find the trouble and to tell the advertiser how to remedy it.

The agent is constantly pointing to larger things. His province is similar to that of the wife of a successful man. She encourages him; she inspires him. She helps him with the little things. Her greatest ambition is that he succeed. But, when he does succeed, she must not claim credit for his accomplishments. His very success depends on the world's recognition of his having done it himself. Many agents have lost accounts which they have developed because of too much "crowing." The advertising agency's first function is that of an adviser. Most agents do not accept competing accounts. They stake their success on the success of the advertiser, and help him fight his battles with his competitors. Just as in the case of the doctor and the lawyer, the more frank one is with his adviser the more intelligent is the advice he receives.

The story is told of a manufacturer with a new product for which he was willing to spend $100,000 in advertising. He called on an agent and asked for advice regarding the best way to spend the money. The agent investigated the product, the possible demand and the competition. He told the manufacturer that in his opinion the investment would not be a profitable one and advised him not to advertise. The manufacturer went to another agent and received the same advice. In all he went to six agencies, ready to place his $100,000 in their hands, and in each case was told to keep his money.

For a time the patent medicine advertisers, the liquor advertisers and a few of the railroads felt that by placing their advertisements direct with the publishers, they were in a better position to influence the editorial columns and to censor news and editorial matter that might hurt their businesses. As the publishers have become stronger in their determination not to let the advertising columns influence the editorial columns, and as the agencies have become Stronger in the volume of business given to the publishers, advertisers have realized that if their claims for or against editorial discrimination are just, the influence of the agency on the publisher is greater than the influence of any individual advertiser could be.

7. *The outsider's viewpoint.* The advice rendered by the agent is valuable, partly because it is based on his own experience, his records of the experiences of others and his knowledge of merchandising methods. But it is valuable also because the agent brings to any advertiser's problems the outsider's viewpoint. It is said that a doctor cannot diagnose his own case. Similarly, a manufacturer becomes involved in the details of his business and in his fight against competition, and it is hard for him to see his business as a part of the great distributive system. The advertising manager represents the business from the inside. The advertising agent represents the public as related to that business. The manufacturer considers his product as something to sell. The agent considers the product as something to buy.

8. *How agencies are organized.* The advertising agency is a group of specialists, each one devoting his life to the study of his branch of the many problems in relation to advertising. Every agency has in theory at least three main divisions:

1. Sales or promotion department
2. A creative or production department for the preparation of advertisements
3. An operating department for the purpose of estimating, ordering, accounting, checking and billing.

The service manager or account executive has constant contact with the advertiser. He is a man experienced in planning advertising campaigns and in merchandising problems. Usually the service manager handles accounts which, while in no way competing, are similar in merchandising problems. For instance, an agency will have service managers each specializing on food, agricultural, mail order, clothing, building material, office appliance and technical machinery advertising. Each one of these men, thru contact with his particular industry, becomes a specialist in that particular division of business and furnishes the production or creative departments with the merchandising information on which to build the campaign.

In most agencies there are five purely creative departments, the copy department, the art department and the material department which make up one group of purely creative function and the research and media departments whose province it is to collect and weigh information for use by the Plan Board.

Agencies are in the habit of calling conferences constantly and usually no new subject is taken up Without having a conference in which each group of specialists is represented. At these conferences the experiences of all of the members of the Plan Board are gathered together and the judgment is a judgment of specialists. The sales manager furnishes his experience from the standpoint of sales; the service manager furnishes his experience from the standpoint of merchandising; the research department furnishes its records from the library and from the results of field investigations; the copy department gives its angle from the standpoint of the psychological appeal; the art department states whether or not the idea may be visualized and presents rough sketches of its suggestions as to the best plan of presenting the message in the most attractive form; the material department, whose duty it is to prepare the engravings, the composition, the printing and the electrotypes, considers the problem in relation to its mechanical limitations and the media department furnishes information as to the most economical media in relation to circulation and the past experience of the agency.

9. *How an agency works.* The chart, on page 320, shows the simplest steps undertaken by the average agency in conducting an advertising campaign for a client. The four main steps are:
   A. Investigating or obtaining all the information necessary in order to make an intelligent plan
   B. Planning
   C. Producing or creating the advertisements

D. Operating or taking care of the financial side of the transaction and recording results.

The conscientious advertising agent will make no recommendations until the organization has made a complete study of the problem. He does not even answer hypothetical questions, to say nothing of writing copy and preparing sketches, until every source of information has been tapped and all of the information so obtained has been carefully analyzed. Not only, as said, do very few agencies accept competing accounts but most agencies exercise the greatest care and the utmost caution in selecting clients for whom they are to conduct campaigns.

Before active solicitation has commenced, the members of the agency, usually the manager of sales, the president of the company, and the service manager who would handle the account, as well as the credit than of the agency, have a conference as to the desirability of the account and the possibility for success. In some organizations definite action is taken by the New Business Board before an account is solicited.

10. *Obtaining information for the campaign.* When the sales manager has closed the contract with the client, he then introduces the agency's service manager who is to have charge of the account. This officer proceeds to make arrangements for the investigation. Many agencies have a definite outline of questions which in most cases will furnish the information desired. These lists of questions are much like the diagnosis sheet of a physician. They scrutinize every detail of the client's business and weigh each with respect to competition. There are four sources from which the agency obtains answers to the inquiries that compose its questionnaire.

First, the client's own organization, and before complete answers are secured the agency will have interviewed the heads of most of the departments. The second step in investigating is to gather together all of the information in the agency's library in relation to the particular industry. Here the agency has indexed records of all successful advertising campaigns conducted in that industry. It also has information in relation to specific markets and the number and kind of distributors. After the library investigation, the head of the research department and the service manager who is to handle the account determine on whatever field investigations may be necessary. These consist of calls on consumers, dealers, distributors and other groups which influence sales in an effort to obtain their answers to the same fundamental questions. At the same time that the field investigation is being conducted, the agency is gathering together proofs of all advertisements of the client and of his competitors, records of the advertising which each has done in the past and records of the follow-up which each conducts on each group to which the advertising is directed.

11. *Planning the campaign.* When the research department has furnished the results of these four kinds of investigations to the service manager, he then asks for a meeting of the Plan Board and presents the findings. The details of the plan may differ with recounts and may differ with agencies. Some prefer to make the illustrations first; others prefer to write the copy before having it illustrated. Still others prefer a combination of both methods, writing only one piece of copy to show style. At the plan conference the dominant idea of each class advertising is determined and the Plan Board decides on the size of space and the number of insertions which will be required in the campaign. In some agencies, the service manager writes all the copy. Most agencies, however, have a copy department with this duty as a sole function. In such cases, the copy department takes the dominant idea and prepares a list of advertisement subjects for each advertisement. Before any copy is written the advertisement subjects are approved by the service manager and by the manager of production. Then the advertisement subjects are submitted to the art department for rough layouts or "visualizations" of the idea. The finished copy and the finished art work is not ordered until the client has approved the idea of the copy and illustration and most agencies at this step also estimate the cost for the purchase of art work, cuts and composition.

That there may be no misunderstanding, the advertising plan is usually put on paper. After the plan has been read to and approved by the Plan Board, it is submitted to the client together with the findings of the investigation. This is the most important function of the agency and usually takes the greater part of the time. One agency finds that on the average at least three months must be consumed in investigating, one month in planning and two months in producing before the right kind of advertisements can be completed. This is one of the many reasons why a year's campaign is planned at one time.

12. *Producing the advertisements.* When the client has approved the plan, the agency proceeds to order the space. The layouts are then sent to the artist who, because of his particular technique or knowledge in relation to the class of illustration desired, has been chosen to prepare the drawings. The artist first

submits pencil sketches and when these are approved the layouts are sent to the copy department for the writing of the copy. By this method the copywriter knows that the subject of each advertisement is exactly the subject which the client desires because it has been approved by the client and, having the layout in front of him, can consider the advertisement from the standpoint of the reader who sees the illustration and he can also make his copy fit the space which has been agreed upon and which is available in the layout.

When the finished drawings are received, they are submitted to the client, together with the copy, and after the client's approval the production is simply a matter of the detail of ordering cuts, setting the advertisement, making a sufficient number of proofs in the case of a publication advertisement or printing in case of a booklet or circular, preparing one plate, an electrotype, stereotype or matrix for each advertisement in each publication and shipping the plates to the publisher.

13. *Relation of agency to advertiser.* There has been much discussion about the division of functions between the advertising agent and the advertiser's own advertising department. In some cases, as was shown in the last chapter, advertisers have attempted to get along without advertising departments of their own, making the agency responsible for all details of the campaign. In other cases, the advertiser has an extensive advertising department, and uses the agency chiefly for counsel to aid in the copy writing and to place the advertisements in publications. Between these two extremes there is every shade of variation in practice. In theory, the advertising manager of a business and the advertising agent with whom he works should confer on all important matters, the advertising manager bringing to the conference the facts regarding the business, its goods, its personnel and its policies, and the agent bringing the outsider's viewpoint with a detailed knowledge of advertising principles and media and a fund of data regarding merchandising plans and methods.

The agent's plans and his suggested methods of carrying them out are subject to the approval of the advertising manager or of some other responsible member of the advertiser's organization. A spirit of mutual helpfulness and a common and unselfish desire really to advance the interests of the advertiser will do more to bring the advertising manager and the agent into helpful cooperation than any amount of cut-and-dried rules defining their respective functions.

14. **The advertising agent's compensation.** In a sense the advertising agency is the middleman in the advertising business. He does not buy space in large quantities to resell in smaller quantities, nevertheless he does sell space for the publisher. For this service he is paid by the publisher. The ordinary service rendered by the agent to his principal-study of the client's business, the writing of copy, and the placing of copy, etc.—costs the advertiser nothing. That is, the advertiser could not buy space any more cheaply if he performed these services for himself, than he can buy it and also utilize the agency.

The space used by the advertiser is billed to him by the agent generally at the publisher's card rates. The publisher bills the agent for the space used by his client, at the card rate less a certain differential, and it is this differential that represents the agent's gross compensation. Out of it he has to pay all the expenses of conducting his agency, keeping what remains as profit. The differential allowed by the majority of magazine publishers is fifteen per cent. That is, if an advertiser uses one thousand dollars' worth of space in a publication, the publisher bills the agent for the full amount less 15 per cent and allows 2 per cent of the net for cash. The agent in turn bills the advertiser in one of two ways. The usual way is to bill for the full figure but allow the amount of the discount that has previously been given the agent by the publisher—2 per cent of the publisher's net being 1.7 percent of the agent's bill to the advertiser. The other way of billing an advertiser is at the publisher's net less 2 per cent for cash and then charging 15 per cent for service. The second way gives the agency about $25 less on $1,000.

While to one unfamiliar with the advertising business the agency's commission may appear to be in every involved condition, as a matter of fact it is less involved and rates are more rigidly adhered to than in almost any other class of business. An agent who cuts rates is regarded as an outlaw, and he may at any moment lose recognition from the publishers and will not be allowed membership (or will be expelled from membership) in the American Association of Advertising Agencies.

The agency's commission, allowed him by those who control advertising media, pays for the ordinary agency service. Many agencies make an additional "service charge" to advertisers when the services rendered involve unusual outlays of money.

Some agencies make a preliminary charge for the investigation and others charge for the investigation and the plan, whether the advertiser uses it or not. In some cases, after the investigation is made it is found that there is not a sufficient market for the product, in which case the advertiser pays the agent on a time basis or an estimated sum for the work involved. The advertiser also pays the agent a 15% service fee on all material purchases made for the advertiser. These include drawings, cuts, printing and all other such items. Thus the average agency works on a straight 15% basis.

It usually costs the agency from 10 to 13% to render this service, thus the agent makes from 2 to 5% on his money. Agencies pride themselves on never missing a cash discount and usually make the taking of the cash discount a part of the contract with the advertiser. It is obvious, under such a close margin, that an agency cannot extend credit. If an agency makes a net profit of 3% it is only making $300 a month profit on an account which is spending $10,000 a month in publications. If the agency had to pay the publisher for one month's advertising on which it received no remuneration from the advertiser, it would have to handle a volume of business in the relation that $300 is to $10,000 before it would break even on this loss. This means that an agency would have to do $333,000 worth of business in order to make up one month of a $10,000 billing. If the advertiser defaulted for two months, the agency would have to do $666,000 worth of billing and so the loss would increase each month. The agency, being responsible to the publisher for the debts of the advertiser and working on such a small margin, insists on prompt payment, takes no notes and reserves the right to cancel immediately advertising whenever there is any question of the advertiser's ability to pay. In case of such cancelation, however, it is also agreed that the advertiser pay the agent for the amount of work which he has put on the advertisements which would have appeared in the space so canceled.

15. **The meaning of "recognition."** Several times in the preceding paragraphs we have referred to "recognition" of agencies by publishers. An advertising agency is "recognized" when the publisher grants a commission for advertising received from the agency. As advertising agencies began to increase in number and to demand of publishers statements of circulation and fixed rates for space, the publishers found it advisable to organize associations to investigate the standing and responsibility of the agents in order that the publishers might be protected from the unscrupulous and the irresponsible. The newspapers have performed this function thru the American Newspaper Publishers Association, the magazines thru

the Periodical Publishers Association, and the farm journals have another organization of their own. There are some publishers who will not grant recognition until they, individually, have made a special contract with the agent.

These associations demand of the advertising agent a satisfactory financial statement, a record of the past experience and accomplishments of the individuals in charge of the agency, an assurance that the agency will not rebate any of its commissions to the advertisers, a list of the accounts, and in some cases a statement of the volume of business which the agency is prepared to place. The number of accounts necessary to secure recognition varies. While the associations generally adhere to the rule that an agency must have at least three accounts, in some cases a publisher insists upon at least three accounts placed in his publication; and all now demand that the agency be entirely free, on a financial basis, from the advertiser.

16. *How an agency secures recognition.* With so many organizations from which an agency must obtain recognition before it can do business profitably, it is a difficult matter for the new agency to secure satisfactory recognition. When one considers the credit risk the publishers take, it is right that an agency's ability should be carefully tested before recognition is granted.

From the advertiser's viewpoint, it is important that the advertising agent with whom he deals should be recognized by all classes of media. This arises from the fact that the agent's compensation comes chiefly in the form of commissions from publishers. If he were granted a commission by one publisher and not by another, he might be suspected of putting his own interests before his client's if he were to select the first publisher's periodical, and not the second's, as a proper medium for his client's advertisements. That most agents, however, do not let the matter of commissions influence their advice to their clients is indicated by the many cases in which conscientious advertising agencies have placed large volumes of business with certain publishers who did not grant them recognition.

To insure to the agent proper compensation from all media that his clients' campaigns may require, as well as to avoid other difficulties in the methods of recognition in vogue in the past, a new plan of agency recognition was proposed by the American Association of Advertising Agencies in 1921. The plan comprehends joint recognition by all media, the recognition to be granted by a central body, one representative from each medium and one from the Agents' Association. This will give the new agency an opportunity to start on an equal basis with respect to all media, and will give each medium and the agents themselves an equal voice in the recognition of others to their ranks.

The new plan will do much to clear up the agency situation, and, while it may not be easier under it to secure recognition for an agency, it certainly will allow those securing recognition to do business on a more satisfactory basis; it should aid publishers, advertisers and agencies alike.

ADVISORY 5

ADVERTISING MEDIA

1. *Place of the medium in the campaign.* We have discussed the demand for the product, the possible market, the competition and the men who conduct the advertising campaign. Our next question is: How may the advertisements be brought before the public? What instrument or instruments are we to use to send our advertising message to the greatest number of potential customers?

In advertising, as in war, the men who direct the forces are constantly confronted by the problem of choosing the best means of carrying on the campaign operations. What media are to be used? For any given product, designed to reach a given class of people, what means can best serve the advertiser in carrying his message to the people he wants to reach? Shall it be magazines or newspapers, street cars, circular letters, catalogs, sampling, house organs or painted signs, electrical displays, demonstrations and so on to the end of a long list? We are to find that there are three main classes of media, direct media, periodicals, signs,—just as there are three main divisions of an army, infantry, cavalry and artillery, and that these three advertising classes divide and subdivide into so many groups that the problem of selecting the right media is as difficult as it is important.

2. *One medium alone seldom sufficient.* In war few campaigns have succeeded by the use of one branch of the service alone. Napoleon placed too much confidence in his artillery, and this is said to have been one of the causes of his fall at Waterloo. So in advertising, few successes are attributable to the use of only one class of media. Campbell's Soups were first advertised in the street-cars, and for a long time this was the only class of advertising the company used. Today, however, this

great advertiser is depending on magazine advertising for the greater proportion of its success, and is also using newspaper advertising in many localities.

The choice of the media to be used is one of the most important problems of any advertising campaign.

3. *Advertising media defined*. An advertising medium, in its broadest sense, is any vehicle which carries an advertising message, suggestion or impression. Everyone in business at some time in his career has had someone try to sell him something on the ground that "it will be a good 'ad' for you." The doctor and the lawyer, who are usually left alone by the advertising solicitor, are persuaded to buy expensive automobiles, fine homes and memberships in clubs on the pretext of "advertising." The politician buys space in the program which the ladies of the church are going to use at their next fair. Each of these methods carries a suggestion or makes an impression on the public. The impression is valuable or not according to its character and its intensity. Generally its value is far below what could be secured thru the so-called legitimate or regular media, like the mails, periodicals and signs, but not always.

Mr. M. W. Savage of the International Stock Food Company owned Dan Patch, Minor Heir and other famous horses. The name of Dan Patch was inseparable from the International Stock Food Company, and wherever he appeared he was an advertisement for his owner and his owner's business.

4. *How media are selected*. At the outset of a study of media the advertiser should clearly understand that all media are good. They are not all good for all purposes or for all advertisers, but each one for some particular purpose and in some particular way can perform a useful service for some advertiser. There are many rival claims of superiority among the people who try to induce advertisers to use different classes of media. Some magazine men try to convince advertisers that magazines as a class are better media than newspapers, and then the newspaper publishers set up counter claims of superiority for their publications. Billboards are said to be better than street-car cards, and street-car cards are said to be better than billboards. And so the fruitless controversy goes on respecting all kinds of media. Such discussion is as futile as to debate the relative value to man of baseball, golf and tennis.

One class of media is not better than another. It may be better for a certain purpose, and worse for another. The problem of the advertiser is, first, to find out definitely what purpose he wants to achieve—what people he wants to reach, what he wants them to do, how his product can best be made to appeal to them, how they live, earn, spend and play—and then to pick out, after unprejudiced consideration of all media, the ones that can best carry his message about his product to his market. The problem is individual for each advertiser.

5. *Circulation.* The circulation of any advertisement is, in its broadest sense, the number of individuals who may be expected to see it. The circulation of a medium is the number of people that it reaches. How it reaches them: whether by newsstand sale, or subscription, and if the latter on what inducement, we are not here to discuss. At this point, however, it is important to emphasize the fact that circulation does not always or often mean the actual number of people who see an advertisement—it means the number who may be expected to see it. The user of direct media sends out 5,000 form letters. His circulation is 5,000. One thousand or more of his letters may go into the waste-basket of recipients without being read. It is the advertiser's task to make his direct advertising so attractive in appearance that most or every one of his 5,000 circulation will really see and read his message. The user of periodicals may buy a circulation of 100,000. That is what he pays for. He does not necessarily, however, purchase 100,000 readers of his advertisement. Whether any or all of the people who make up the 100,000 circulation of his media see and read his advertisement depends on his ability to attract their attention and to arouse their interest. In other words, circulation and readers of an advertisement are two separate and altogether distinct things. Circulation is a mechanical thing that can be bought. Readers cannot be bought; they must be persuaded.

Until recent years statements of circulation have often been unreliable. Some publishers refused to give any statements regarding circulation, and others were satisfied with round numbers that were obviously inaccurate. The sellers of space for signs made little effort to estimate the number of people who might see them, and even users of direct advertising bought lists of names with frequent disregard for their timeliness and value. Now, all this is changed. Sworn circulations are the order of the day. Circulation is a matter of careful investigation, and everyone publishers, billboard people, companies controlling streetcar space, advertisers and the government itself—is concerned with the circulation of advertising media. The United States Post Oflice Department demands sworn statements of circulation from newspapers, and the Audit Bureau of Circulation to which most periodical publishers, advertisers and agents belong, issues detailed analyses of circulation for its members. Other associations and individuals are rendering similar service. This is decidedly the day of known circulations.

6. *Three general classes of media.* All advertising media may be divided into three classes:

    a. *Direct media*—thru which the possible customer is reached directly by the advertiser, either by mail or by some other distributing agency fully controlled by the advertiser.

    b. *Periodicals*—thru which the possible customer is reached, indirectly, thru publishers.

    c. *Signs*—thru which the possible customer is reached in his travel about town or the country.

In the case of direct media, the circulation is entirely in the hands of the advertiser. He makes up his own list of possible customers and reaches them for the most part thru the mail. He may add a name or eliminate a name at will. He is in full control of all advertising media of this class.

When one buys space in a periodical he does not have full control of its circulation. The publisher comes to the advertiser and announces that he is distributing his publication regularly to a certain class of readers. He offers to introduce the advertiser to these readers thru space in his publication. He tells the advertiser the class of readers he can reach. The advertiser can pick and choose his publications, but he has no control over the circulation of these publications.

Signs include a wide variety of different kinds of media. Neither the advertiser nor the one who sells the space has full control of the circulation reached by signs. An electric sign may be placed at the corner of Broadway and Forty-Second Street in New York. Estimates, based on careful count, can be made of the number of people who will pass that point every twenty-four hours, but the advertiser cannot buy a definite circulation for the sign. It will vary from day to day and week to week according to the habits of the people. The second party in the advertising triangle, the shifting public, determines the circulation.

7. *Kinds of direct media.* Each of the three classes of media divides itself into six kinds, making eighteen in all. While the division may be somewhat arbitrary it will simplify perplexing questions. If the reader will consider the media used by any specific business in relation to the chart printed in the Appendix, page 321, he will find that there is a place and a reason for each kind.

The seven kinds of direct media are

1. Letters
2. Sampling and demonstration
3. Booklets
4. Catalogs
5. House organs
6. Novelties.
7. Internet

8. *Letters.* The first kind of direct media is the duplicated letter. A letter written to one individual and sent only to him is properly not advertising at all. It is personal salesmanship, because presumably the personal characteristics of the recipient were appealed to when the letter was dictated. A letter that is duplicated, however, and that goes to a group of people, is properly called advertising, because it is an appeal to a group rather than to an individual.

9. *Sampling and demonstrating.* In sampling or demonstrating, the actual thing to be sold is allowed to speak for itself. In a sense, sampling and demonstrating are a form of personal salesmanship rather than of advertising, because the article to be sold is usually put personally into the hands of the possible purchaser. Nevertheless, these publicity methods are usually classed as advertising because every sample in a lot of ten thousand is usually distributed in exactly the same way as every other sample; the appeal is really a mass appeal, Although the samplers come into actual contact with individuals.

10. *Booklets.* The next group of direct media includes booklets, leaflets and folders. Some advertising campaigns are built entirely on two direct media, sampling and either booklets, leaflets or folders. The booklet tells the story more completely than it can be told in a letter. In the booklet one can show illustrations, while this is difficult in a letter. The booklet is one step farther removed from the

salesman. It has been said that every advertising campaign calls for at least one booklet. No letter, periodical or sign can tell the whole story.

11. *Catalogs.* The next general group of direct advertising media consists of catalogs. The advertising of Sears, Roebuck & Company is confined to catalogs almost exclusively. In the beginning of the business this company was a large user of space in periodicals. The number of customers finally became so great, and the company obtained such direct connections with its patrons that all periodical advertising was discontinued, and the catalog is today the only kind of advertising used. The following explanation of his company's advertising policy was made by Mr. Richard W. Sears a few years before his death:

We have simply outgrown the circulation of mail-order journals, farm and religious papers, magazines, and similar mediums, because long use of them to advertise our catalog has given the book a wider distribution than any periodicals we can use. What periodical has a circulation of 5,000,000 copies? Yet we put out that many catalogs a year. Every twenty-four hours 12,000 requests for the book come to us, and we are sending out, at the same time, later editions to people already on the mailing lists. There is no duplication in this circulation. We take every precaution to see that no person gets two copies of the catalog the same year. Every name and address to which a copy is sent is filed geographically and every request is compared with this file. When the business was new, we advertised the catalog persistently, but now we do not advertise it at all. Yet we send out nearly 100,000 copies every week. Of the requests that come seventy-five per cent are from people who have an old catalog. Only twenty-five percent are new.

Matters have gone on to a stage where periodical advertising no longer pays us, because there are not enough new prospects left in the country to make it profitable.

We can't see how to spend more money profitably in periodicals. Our catalog tells our story so effectively that no amount of newspaper or magazine space could produce the same advertising effect.

Despite this condition in rural districts, when Sears, Roebuck & Company attempts to extend its field, as it has done in selling a special edition of the Encyclopedia Britannica, it is a most liberal user of both magazine and newspaper space. In such cases the mail-order house advertises to reach a new market which its catalog does not reach and in which its catalog alone does not carry sufficient prestige.

Few advertisers can rely solely on the catalog, because few of them have covered their field as intensively as the big mail-order houses. The catalog is usually a supplementary advertising medium, to aid the salesman and to turn into orders inquiries produced by other kinds of advertising media.

12. *House organs*. A house organ is a publication, usually in the form of a magazine or newspaper, issued by a business house in the interests of that house. It appears, ordinarily, at regular intervals, and, therefore, it might be thought of as a periodical instead of a direct medium. It is properly classified as a direct medium because, regardless of when it appears, its' circulation is entirely in the control of the advertiser.

House organs are of many different kinds.

The house organ that acts as a direct advertising medium is the one that goes to dealers or to consumers. Many manufacturers publish more or less elaborate magazines, in the interest of their own business which they send regularly to jobbers and retailers as well as to the traveling salesmen and clerks of these distributors. Other advertisers, dealing direct with consumers, send regularly their sales story in the form of magazines of varying degrees of pretentiousness to people who might be interested. House organs are ordinarily used to back up the work of salesmen and the appeal of other kinds of advertising; very seldom are they used alone.

13. *Novelties*. The next class of direct media is known as novelties or specialties. It consists of calendars, pocketbooks, knives, paper weights and a large variety of other articles of more or less utility to the one to whom they are presented. Novelties are usually given away by the advertiser, Although sometimes the possible customer is asked to pay a nominal price for them. A novelty is ordinarily something that will be constantly before the recipient and which will, therefore, continually remind him of the advertiser. Another element of value is supposed to lie in the fact that the recipient of a novelty, if it is of any value, will feel a degree of gratitude to the advertiser, and will reciprocate by giving him his orders.

Some novelties have still another kind of value. They result in the good-will of the recipient, but they also act as signs to draw the attention of others. Nearly everyone has seen the watch charm in the form of a green pickle, given away by the manufacturer of Heinz pickles. This is valued by the man who wears it, and it also serves to advertise Heinz pickles to others. In the same class are umbrellas and horse blankets which carry advertising. Probably the most effective advertising specialties are those that serve both as signs and as direct media.

ADVISORY 6

ADVERTISING MEDIA (Continued)

1. *Periodicals.* The second main division of advertising media, called periodicals or publications, may be subdivided into six general groups:

1. Newspapers
2. General magazines
3. Farm papers

4. Trade, technical, and class publications
5. Foreign language publications
6. Directories and miscellaneous periodicals

2. *Newspapers.* Newspapers as a class carry more advertising than any other one medium. They carried advertising before the modern magazine made its appearance, and they continue as exceedingly important advertising aids, not alone for the local dealer, but for the manufacturer as well. It is not possible accurately to define the term newspaper, because the dividing line between some newspapers and some magazines is exceedingly indistinct. However, a description is as good as a definition for our purposes, and ordinarily a newspaper has certain characteristics which permit of its easy classification.

There are two outstanding characteristics. First, a newspaper is concerned chiefly with the printing of news-not the news of special trades or interests, but the general news of the community and the world. Second, a newspaper ordinarily serves a definite locality. It may have subscribers all over the country, but the bulk of its readers are found in the community in which it is published.

Newspapers may be classified in a variety of ways. Using the interval between issues as the basis of classification, we have dailies, weeklies, semi-weeklies and perhaps others. Few real newspapers are published less frequently than once a week. Another basis of classification gives morning, evening and Sunday papers.

We are not now concerned with the sub classifications. The important thing is that the newspaper is primarily a local medium, of undoubted value for the advertiser who wishes to reach intensively the buying public of a given community.

3. *Magazines*. A magazine differs from a newspaper chiefly in that it is not primarily concerned with the printing of news. It may summarize the news (for example, The Outlook, The Independent and The Literary Digest), but its chief purpose is to comment on the news and to interpret it, or to instruct and amuse with fiction, essays and other forms of more or less permanent literature. Although some magazines are published for a local clientele, most of them circulate rather widely in a state, a section, or throughout the entire country.

Magazines are variously classified. First, there are the weeklies, monthlies, quarterlies and annuals; some are published twice a week, others every two weeks and a very few at still other intervals. Magazines are also classified on the basis of their readers; for example, publications for men, for women, for children. A publication might be intended only for a particular group of people—those belonging to a certain religious denomination, for instance. Strictly speaking, such a publication, judged by its contents, might be a magazine even with this limited audience. In the language of advertising, however, it would be a class publication and not a magazine, the latter word being arbitrarily reserved for periodicals with a relatively wide appeal.

4. *Farm journals*. Farm journals reach people in rural communities. Farm journals are for the most part territorial in their influence and the circulation does not extend beyond certain agricultural belts. There are, for instance, corn-belt farm papers and wheat-belt farm papers. Other farm papers concentrate their circulation in certain states. For instance, there are three farm papers published in Minnesota. About seventy per cent of the circulation of the two leaders is in Minnesota with the remainder in North and South Dakota, Montana, western Wisconsin and northern Iowa. There are, however, at least six national farm papers, which advertisers use to reach farmers all over the country in the same way that they use the national magazines to reach generally the inhabitants of cities and towns throughout the United States. The farm journals of this country have probably done as much as any other one influence to introduce better farming.

They have gone hand in hand with the agricultural colleges and the United States Department of Agriculture in their great educational work.

5. *Trade, technical and class publications.* A periodical, to be classed as a trade, technical or class publication, must be edited so as to appeal to a certain group of people possessing common interests. A trade publication, technically speaking, is one that is devoted to the business interest of dealers in merchandise. The Dry Goods Economist is an example; it reaches owners and buyers of dry-goods stores and department stores. Many trade papers are exceedingly influential and are valued for advertisers who wish to reach dealers. Almost every line of business has its trade paper, and in some lines there are many competing publications.

A technical publication is ordinarily one that goes to consumers, instead of to dealers, and is devoted to the interests of those engaged in a technical activity. For example, The Engineering and Mining Journal is a technical periodical reaching mining engineers and others interested in the technical side of mining. Similarly, The American Medical Journal is a technical publication for physicians.

Class publications are periodicals appealing to a certain class of people, and not properly included among either trade or technical publications. Every religious denomination has its own class periodicals—about 1,200 in the United States. Printers' Ink is a class publication appealing to those interested in advertising, Although it might almost be classed as a technical periodical. Every large social group or association has its class paper. There are also class publications for the rural district, such as American Fruit Grower and Hoard's Dairyman.

6. *Foreign language publications.* Another large group of publications is found in the foreign language field. In a sense they are class publications. There are nearly 1,300 publications in the United States printed in foreign languages. America is the great melting pot, and while the first occupation of the new American is usually that of learning the language, there are many who speak English and cannot read it. These people can often be reached only thru the foreign language publications, which are for the most part published weekly, Although many appear daily and are usually newspapers in form and purpose.

7. *Directories.* The next class of publications includes directories and miscellaneous periodicals. Directories include city directories, telephone directories, trade directories and all other periodical publications to which one

refers when in search of names, numbers or other similar information. Advertisements in such publications are usually little more than display cards announcing the business of the advertisers. Some of the important directories which appeal to special interests sell space on the basis of a guaranteed circulation and in them advertisements are more diversified in character.

8. *Theater programs.* Among the remaining publications that appear periodically, theater programs are perhaps most important for the advertiser. They are widely used for a certain type of advertising appeal to which a theater audience is supposed to be peculiarly responsive. The control of theater program advertising in the larger cities is now in the hands of a syndicate, so that it is possible for an advertiser to place a single contract for theater program space in a number of cities from coast to coast.

9. *Signs.* The sign is probably the oldest form of advertising. The Egyptians and Romans were nations of sign users. Among the ruins of Herculaneum and Pompeii there still exist signs carved in stone to advertise the wares of bakers and vintners and the services of hair-dressers. Modern signs are of six classes, with many subdivisions in each class. The six main groups are:

1. Dealers' signs
2. Posters
3. Painted bulletins
4. Electrical signs
5. Street-car cards
6. Theater signs

10. *Dealers' signs.* Dealers' signs include all signs in or about the place where the article advertised is sold, distributed or manufactured. They include also the dealer's name over the door or in some other prominent place on the outside of the store. Usually such a sign is a simple announcement: "John Jones, Grocer." Some manufacturers have found it to their advantage to furnish permanent signs of this sort to dealers for the privilege of adding at the end "Buy Arbuckle's Coffee Here," or some other such phrase. Many advertisers supply similar signs for the window sills of stores. Then there are window trims, counter signs, wall signs and special display racks bearing the advertisement of the manufacturer who furnishes them.

11. *Posters*. The poster is an out-of-doors advertisement printed on sheets of paper and pasted on flat display surfaces. Until a few years ago, posters were pasted on fences or any other available flat surface with or without the permission of the owners. Today the poster plants of the country have established standard sizes of boards and rent all their locations. The standard poster sheet is twenty-eight by forty-two inches, and a single poster "stand" is made up of eight, twelve, sixteen or twenty-four sheets. The height of a poster is nine and one-fourth feet. The twenty-four-sheet poster is now becoming recognized as the standard size, giving a display twenty-one feet long by nine and one-fourth feet high. The different showings are graded by the class of boards on which they are displayed. The grades are AA, A, B, C, and D. The D board is a wooden structure without a frame. The AA board is a steel structure with a green molding frame and several inches of white paper or "blanking" around the sheets. Poster advertising rates are based on the month of display, and the price varies with localities.

12. *Painted bulletins*. The next general group of signs includes all kinds of painted bulletins. Painted bulletins are much like posters in purpose and in the kinds of things that can be profitably advertised on them; but, of course, painted bulletins are much less widely used because each bulletin must be separately painted, and skilled men are required to produce them. Painted bulletin advertising, for the most part, is confined to the larger cities and to positions along the main traveled roads. Few of the smaller towns are equipped to furnish painted bulletins.

Painted bulletins may roughly be divided into three classes:

1. City boards
2. Railroad boards
3. Painted walls

The twenty-live-foot bulletin has for a long time been considered standard, although of late many advertisers are using fifty-foot boards both in the city and in the country. Contracts are generally made on a three years' basis.

In cities, where the buildings are high and crowded together, few walls are available for painted display advertising, and those that are available are consequently high in price. Painted display advertisements showing to streets having a heavy night traffic may profitably be lighted at night by means of electric reflecting light. The price for signs includes the cost of painting, illuminating and maintenance. Lighted walls are usually sold on a flat rate per month based on the expense for rent, painting and illumination; this expense varies for different localities.

13. *Electric signs.* "The Great White Way" derives its name and fame from the electric advertising signs that illuminate it. In New York, upper Broadway at night is one of the sights of the metropolis. This is the electric sign center of the country. The number and effectiveness of the electric signs there and elsewhere prove that electric signs are one of the great advertising media.

Electric signs are ordinarily composed of sheet steel letters mounted on steel frames, each letter being lighted by a strip of incandescent electric bulbs by means of what are known as "flashers"—mechanical contrivances that automatically turn on and shut off the electric current. The copy and illustrations on these signs are frequently made to change at intervals, and possess great attractive value thru a combination of color, motion and pleasing design. Every important city in the United States has many of these electric signs. The price is hard to estimate, as each stand is sold separately. Signs are usually lighted from dusk until after midnight each evening. Some advertisers have set aside the greater part of their appropriations for this class of advertising media.

14. *Railway signs.* Advertising in street cars, elevated trains and subways has grown with the marvelous development of urban and interurban transportation. This class of advertising includes cards in the cars as well as bulletins on the station platforms. The "circulation" of this class of advertising media can be measured much more readily than that of any other kind of signs. The companies controlling street-car, elevated and subway advertising obtain from the transportation companies records of the fares collected, and the cost of space is based to an extent on these figures.

The standard street-car card is twenty-one by eleven inches, and one of the arguments in favor of the medium is the fact that each advertiser is given the same size of display. Contracts are made for one year as a minimum, two, three or five years. In many localities the six months' contract is being eliminated, and effort is made to induce the advertiser to contract on the five-year basis, because it has been found that more five-year contracts are renewed than contracts for any other period. Most of the space in street cars is now sold by one organization, the Street Railway Advertising Association. The prices in each community depend on the number of street cars in operation. An advertiser buys a "full run," which means a space in all the cars, or a "half run," which means that his cards appear in half of the cars. Ten years ago some advertisers used double space in "half runs" instead of single space in "full runs." Double space, however, is no longer sold; all advertisers are given equal opportunity for display.

Street-car advertising differs from most other sign advertising in the fact that the public sees the display at a time when it has very little else to do except to read the advertisements. This medium takes advantage of the forced idleness of the street-car passenger at a time when his range of vision is confined to the interior of the car in which he is riding, and when there is little to distract his attention from the message of the advertisers.

15. *Theater signs.* Since the introduction of moving pictures, another great advertising medium has been added. For a long time many theater proprietors have sold display space on their drop curtain, but the theater as a place to reach the masses with advertisements did not fully come into its own until the moving picture brought millions to the houses of amusement regularly. Many ingenious variations of theater advertising have been introduced. The most common is the stereopticon slide which national advertisers furnish to their retail dealers and which the retailers arrange to have displayed in local theaters. Some national advertisers send out to a regular distributing agency moving pictures of their processes of manufacture and the uses of their goods. An expensive campaign of this kind was conducted by the Du Pont Powder Company, showing "Farming With Dynamite."

Films of this nature vary from 250 feet to 1,000 feet in length. The showing of the film is usually arranged either with a film distributing agency or locally with individual picture houses by the advertiser's salesmen or by his dealers.

This medium is still far from standardization. When one central organization can present an advertiser or his agent with definite circulation records of all of the moving picture houses and the cities of varying sizes throughout the country and can guarantee showings on specific dates at the discretion of its advertiser, just as the National Out Door Bureau does for posters and painted bulletins and as the Street Railway Advertising Company does for street car cards, then theater advertising may be purchased intelligently.

There is nothing to prevent the moving picture houses following the lead of the magazines in letting advertising revenue carry part of the editorial burden.

When some genius of organization makes this space available to advertisers on a business basis your moving picture program will be similar to the contents of a magazine-advertising, a comic, a short story, some epigrammatic editorial, the feature story, and then some more advertising.

16. *Why there are not more media.* Every now and then someone thinks that he has discovered a new medium—signs on ice tickets, on bread tickets, in shoe shining parlors or magazine holders, on telephone stands, or in passenger elevators. Why doesn't someone obtain leases for signs on all passenger elevators in America? There is an enormous circulation. The reason is that no one has put the purchase of such space on a business basis of circulation so that it may be bought intelligently in relation to the circulation of other media. That is one reason. The other is that the capital involved in manufacture—gathering the leases, erecting the racks and building up an organization is so great that no one has as yet considered the venture profitable.

ADVISORY 7

WEIGHING CIRCULATION

1. *The value of an advertising medium.* There are two problems in selecting an advertising medium. First, what class of media should be used? Second, in the class or classes chosen, which particular media will aid the most in accomplishing the desired purpose? In this chapter we are to present certain considerations which will help in solving both of these problems. There are some questions to be asked about any class of media before one can properly choose it in an advertising campaign, and there are other questions to be asked and answered about individual media to determine their comparative ability to aid the advertiser. Ordinarily it is not enough to listen to the claims of those who present the merits of different media, there is much that the advertiser or his agent must do to supplement the available data about the different forms of direct media, periodicals and signs before he can be sure that he has selected just the right methods of carrying his advertising message to that part of the public that he wants to reach. The value of any advertising medium is determined mainly by the answers to two questions:

1. What is the cost per possible purchaser reached by the medium?
2. What is the prestige of the medium in the minds of possible purchasers?

Only the first of these questions is considered in the present chapter. It should be noted that this question does not refer to the cost per reader. Cost per reader and cost per possible purchaser are two very different things. If an advertiser wished to know the cost per reader, all he would have to do would be to divide the advertising rate for the unit of space by the number of subscribers and other readers of the publication. A page rate of $1,000, in other words, divided by a proved circulation of 100,000, would give a cost of one cent a page for each reader of the periodical. Unfortunately, however, each reader is not necessarily a possible purchaser of the advertiser's goods, nor does every reader of a medium necessarily see every advertisement in it; therefore it is necessary to consider other things than mere numerical circulation.

2. *Cost per possible purchaser.* Every advertiser must decide how much he can afford to pay to reach every possible purchaser to whom a medium might appeal. This is a difficult matter, the decision varying with each individual case. The factors involved are well illustrated by the answer of an advertising man who was once asked, "If you had only one possible purchaser in the United States, how would you undertake to advertise to him? Would it be advisable to use any advertising under such a circumstance?" He replied: "If I owned a mine valued at $10,000,000 and wished to sell it to one steel magnate in the United States who could afford to buy it, and this man was not approachable in the beginning thru personal salesmanship, I might be willing to spend many thousand dollars in advertising that mine to that one man. My problem would be to study him and to use every advertising medium which would reach him. I should attempt to find his favorite publication, and I could afford to take full pages or even double pages in that publication. If I found that he had no antipathy for signs, I might arrange to have signs placed near his favorite drive, facing his office window, facing his favorite window in his favorite club and every other place where he might be expected to be. I should be willing to spend several thousand dollars on a booklet telling of my mine and of the opportunities it afforded. I should advertise to this man's friends, that they might talk about my mine. In a case of this kind I could afford to spend thousands of dollars per possible purchaser." Fortunately, there is more than one possible purchaser for most advertised articles, but the things to be considered in the selection of media remain the same, regardless of the number of people whom the advertiser hopes to reach. The cost per possible purchaser is not a simple problem; it involves a variety of considerations which have to be correlated and harmonized before the final answer is given.

The advertiser should begin his task of selecting media with the idea, already emphasized in a preceding chapter, that no particular class of media is better than any other particular class. It all depends on the purposes for which the media are to be used. Some are seemingly good for all kinds of advertising campaigns; others are more restricted in their appeal. Whether one medium or another is better for any particular purpose depends on the people the advertiser is trying to reach, the product that he wants to sell and the specific results that he hopes to accomplish with his advertising.

3. *Discovering the typical purchaser.* The first thing to do in selecting media is to have a clear idea of the people to be reached. Who is the typical customer? Advertising is a mass appeal, and separate individuals cannot be appealed to separately. The group alone can be considered, and, before advertising to that group can be successfully undertaken, it is necessary for the advertiser to have a definite idea in his mind of the typical member of the group. Certain questions are to be asked in establishing the characteristics of the typical purchaser, and in the answers to those questions the advertiser often finds that certain media are naturally eliminated from the campaign, and that others naturally present themselves as worthy of consideration. The statement that the advertiser should address his message to the typical purchaser is subject to one qualification. Sometimes the actual purchaser of an article is not the one who really influences the purchase. The head of the household actually buys the piano, the automobile, and the talking machine; yet in very many cases he would never buy these things if he were not influenced to do so by some member of the family. Occasionally the small boy of the family has much to say about the kind of car to be bought; accordingly some automobile manufacturers advertise in boys' magazines. The mother and her daughters usually decide what piano or talking machine is to be purchased; therefore these articles are extensively advertised in women's publications. A few makers of men's clothing, even, have advertised in magazines appealing chiefly to women, in the belief that women often influence their husbands in the matter of buying clothes. The typical purchaser, for the purposes of the advertiser, is the one who induces the purchase of a commodity, no matter whether he or someone else actually furnishes the money to buy it.

4. *Geographical conditions.* First, is the market in which we wish to sell our goods national, territorial or local? If it is restricted to a specific locality, we must choose local media only. Local media are chiefly newspapers and the various kinds of signs. Magazines, on the other hand, are the most commonly used national media. A national campaign, of course, may employ local media as well as those of general circulation.

In a local campaign an advertiser may wish to concentrate his sales and advertising activity in one part of a community. He is helped to do this by some newspapers that divide their statements of circulation so that the advertiser can tell how much of it goes to the city proper, how much to the suburbs and how much to the surrounding country. A few of the larger newspapers even go so far as to indicate on maps the number of copies that go to the various sections of the city. Similarly, in the case of magazines, many publishers now provide statements of circulation by states, to enable the advertiser to choose the medium that goes most intensively into the territory he wants particularly to cultivate. Detailed circulation statements of this sort are required of those publications that are members of the Audit Bureau of Circulations.

In the geographical study of the advertiser's problem the second question is this: Is the typical purchaser to be found in cities, in small towns, or in rural districts? If the purchaser is to be found in the city, the advertiser may use city newspapers, signs, posters, bulletins or street-car cards when the market is local. If it is national, he may use these media together with certain magazines. On the other hand, if his typical possible purchaser is in the small towns, he may use what are known as "small-town magazines," and possibly the country weeklies as well. In the country he must rely chiefly on the agricultural publications. Of course, geographical considerations have nothing to do with the use of direct media. They may be used to reach possible purchasers anywhere.

5. *Social conditions*. As we study our typical purchaser, we see how carefully the different advertising media have planned to reach different groups. The first question in determining the social standing of possible purchasers is: Will the purchase usually be made by men, by women or by children? The second question is: Are the goods intended for the rich, the middle class of people or the poor? There are few commodities that are purchased only by men, or only by women, or only by children. There are few, also, that are purchased only by the rich, the middle class or the poor. The advertiser's problem is to find to which of these classes he is to make most of his sales, and then pick the media that seem to circulate most effectively among those classes. If sales are to be made in any quantity to several classes, he must consider each class as a problem by itself, and pick different kinds of media which will reach the greatest number of possible customers with the least waste circulation.

In fixing the social position of the typical purchaser, the advertiser asks a third question: Is the purchase made by family groups or by individuals? Vacuum cleaners are seldom sold to bachelors in boarding houses. Even tho it might be advisable for educational purposes to advertise certain articles of household use to unmarried people, an advertising medium going only to unmarried people (if there were such a medium) would be of little value in a campaign to sell articles of this sort.

Still another question is this: Is the purchase made by young, middle-aged or old people? A manufacturer considered a certain magazine an ideal medium for him until it was found that the magazine circulated chiefly among the middle-aged, while his product could be sold only to young people. A fashionable tailor, who has the greatest portion of the wealthy trade in a Western city, says: "While the majority of my customers are men of middle age, have you noticed that I advertise only to young men? When a young man begins to consider tailor-made clothing he has passed the age of to-be-a-man-I-must-look-like-papa. He begins to think the old man is a little seedy. Just at that age, also, a father is very proud of his son. I have found that you cannot expect a young man's trade just because you hold his father's trade, but that you can often get the father's trade thru the son."

The advertiser is fortunate who is able to divide and subdivide the people in his market until he has an exact picture of the typical group to which he wishes to talk. Perhaps he is selling only to professional men, or only to clerks, or only to skilled mechanics. Perhaps his product appeals only to mothers, perhaps only to society women. A woman may be both a mother and a society woman. The advertiser must decide to which side of a woman's nature he is to appeal, and pick his media accordingly. If he is advertising to men, he must use media that appeal to those interests of men to which his own product appeals. A magazine dealing with out-door sport, even though circulated only among men, would scarcely be a desirable medium for office furniture. The ideal medium would be one devoted to men's business interests.

For nearly every group of people there is one available medium, and before the advertiser can determine the value of any medium to him he must discover the particular social group to which it makes its appeal.

6. *Circulation statements.* We have been considering questions to be asked and answered by the advertiser in selecting, first, the kind of media to be used, and second, the particular media to be chosen in any class. The remainder of this chapter is concerned chiefly with factors in the comparison of individual media rather than in the selection of broad groups of media for the advertiser's campaign. Geographical and social considerations, in other words, help the

advertiser to decide whether or not to use magazines, and if he is to use magazines, whether to use publications that appeal chiefly to men, women or children; masses or classes, young or old, etc. If he is to use women's magazines, for instance, these considerations also help him somewhat in choosing from the many women's publications covering the fields he wants to reach. There are other things to be considered, however, in selecting individual media in any group. The things to be studied fall chiefly under two heads: circulation (including rates) and prestige.

The problem of finding the exact circulation of a medium is by no means so easy as it may seem. This fact is partly, Although by no means entirely, the reason for the rather slow development of demand on the part of advertisers for exact statements of circulation and of willingness on the part of publishers to comply with these demands. The progress of advertising may be traced by the different stages in the development of accurate and complete statements of circulation.

The circulation of an advertising medium is constantly changing. Even in the case of direct mediums, which are entirely under the control of the advertiser, there is always the "death" rate to be considered. People are constantly moving from place to place, and the list of names must be kept up to date. It is estimated that in ordinary business lines twenty per cent of any mailing list "dies" every year; in other words, twenty per cent of the names or addresses must be eliminated or changed.

Newspapers are largely sold by newsboys on the street, and much of this circulation may be transient. Ninety-eight per cent of the circulation of some magazines is news-stand circulation, and news-stand circulation may or may not mean either the same readers or the same number of readers from month to month.

Even when magazines go chiefly to subscribers, new subscribers are constantly being added to the lists and old subscribers taken off. It was natural, therefore, for publishers to be slow in approaching such a difficult task as the preparation of circulation statements of sufficient accuracy and completeness to make them of any value to the advertiser.

Nevertheless, an advertising rate is necessarily based on the amount of circulation, and advertisers are becoming more and more insistent as to the quantity and quality of the circulation they buy. Circulation statements have in the past been indefinite, and often justly open to suspicion.

7. *History of circulation statements*. In 1868, Mr. George P. Rowell introduced a plan of insuring reliability of circulation statements. Publishers were asked to furnish to him statements of circulation, depositing a forfeit of $100 each. The amount deposited by each publisher was offered as a prize to any person finding his circulation statement to be false.

Another of the early plans looking toward accurate statements of circulation was conceived by a western advertiser, Colonel Emery Mapes of the Cream of Wheat Company. He asked each publication to guarantee a certain amount of circulation on which its rate was based, with the understanding that his own auditors should be allowed to audit the circulation, and that, if it was found not equal to the amount guaranteed, he should be rebated pro rata. This plan was so successful that several magazines later guaranteed their circulation to all advertisers offering a pro rata refund in case the circulation of any issue did not equal the guaranteed circulation on which the advertising rate is based.

Prior to the organization of the Audit Bureau of Circulations there were a number of private auditing associations, many of them performing a useful service. The idea was conceived of bringing all these associations together in one organization composed of publishers, advertising agents and advertisers, the membership dues to be spent in thorough audits of circulation for the common benefit of the members. In this way the Audit Bureau of Circulations was born. Practically all the magazines, farm papers, trade papers and daily newspapers are now members. This solves the problem so far as the publications carrying 80 per cent of the volume of periodical advertising is concerned. There are thousands of weekly papers which are not yet members, however, despite the fact that the minimum membership fee is $50 a year, while the minimum audit costs the bureau $85.

8. *Duplication of circulation*. Most people read more than one magazine or newspaper. The advertiser sometimes finds it advisable to determine to what extent the circulation of the periodicals he is considering is "duplicated"—that is, the number of readers of one medium who are also reached by other mediums. Some advertisers have contended that duplicated circulation is largely waste circulation—that if magazine A and magazine B each has a circulation of 10,000,

and if fifty per cent of the readers of magazine A are also readers of magazine B, the latter medium is not of so much value to an advertiser as magazine C would be, also with 10,000 circulation but reaching a group of readers few of whom are subscribers to magazine A. In this case magazines A and B would be said to have a fifty per cent duplicated circulation.

Duplicated circulation is not necessarily a bad thing; it may be a very good thing, if the advertiser can afford to pay for it. An advertiser conducting an intensive local campaign will use newspapers, street cars, posters and other mediums, with full knowledge that the people who read his advertisements in the newspapers will also be likely to see the street-car cards and his other sign media. He is anxious that they should; he realizes that the average purchaser needs to be influenced many times in many ways before he will buy. In like manner, the intensive advertiser will use several periodical media, many of which are read by the same people, in the well-founded belief that an advertising appeal that comes several times to the attention of the reader will be more effective than if it came before him only once. The intensive advertiser further realizes that an advertisement in a single medium may not even be seen by many readers of that medium, while, if it appears in several media, the reader who subscribes for all of them will be likely to see the advertisement at least once.

Every advertiser, however, cannot be an intensive advertiser. A man with a limited appropriation may find it more advisable to reach 20,000 people by using two magazines, each with a 10,000 circulation, than to reach only 15,000 by using two other magazines, each with a circulation of 10,000, but with a fifty per cent duplication. To advertisers of this sort, and also to advertisers who wish to cultivate their field intensively but who properly wish to control the degree of intensity of their advertising efforts, the problem of duplication in circulation is an important one.

9. *Extent of duplication.* There is much duplicated circulation among all media. Scarcely any two mediums can be found, no matter how widely different they may be in kind and appeal, that do not show some duplication of circulation. It is estimated that there are not over 10,000,000 people in the United States who read the class of media technically known as magazines, and yet the total circulation of all magazines reported by the American Newspaper Annual for 1920 was 44,706,308. The number of people reading magazines is increasing fast, certainly much more rapidly than the population of the country. In 1905 the total

circulation of magazines was 15,122,000, while in 1910 it was 25,512,000. The duplication of circulation is probably increasing at fully as fast a rate.

The most extensive investigation of the duplication of circulation yet conducted was made under the auspices of the Association of National Advertisers in the summer of 1914. It was found that the circulation of some magazines duplicated the circulation of others to the extent of almost fifty per cent. For instance, the Ladies' Home Journal was found to duplicate with the Saturday Evening Post to the extent of forty-two per cent. The percentage of duplication in most cases, however, was very much lower than this.

A similar inquiry in regard to newspapers was made by Professor Walter Dill Scott among 4,000 business and professional men in Chicago. The replies show that in round numbers:

14 per cent read but one newspaper
46 per cent read two newspapers
21 per cent read three newspapers
17 per cent read four or more newspapers
84 per cent read more than one newspaper

The same advertisement seen in two or three newspapers is certainly more effective than if seen in one, but some advertisers are convinced that it is not worth three times as much to have an advertisement seen in three papers, reaching largely the same readers, as it is to have it seen in one.

10. *Subscription price as barometer of purchasing power.* Some people contend that the buying power of a consumer can be determined partly by the amount he pays for a periodical. It is maintained, for instance, that the buying power of readers of magazines, as a class, is greater than the buying power of the average reader of a newspaper. This is probably true; there may be some people who hesitate to pay twenty-five cents for a magazine and yet they can and do pay two or three cents for a newspaper. It is probably true, also, that the readers of a three cent newspaper have a greater individual purchasing power than the average reader of a cheaper newspaper. It is not safe to apply this principle too generally, however. Certain magazines sell for thirty-five and fifty cents a copy; possibly their readers represent greater average purchasing power than the readers of a cheap fiction magazine; this is by no means certain, however, because ministers,

teachers and others with relatively small incomes are found in large numbers on the subscription list of the more expensive periodicals, while popular priced fiction circulates as extensively among families of wealth as among the less well-to-do classes.

A better guide to buying power of readers than the cost of the periodical is a careful study of the contents of the magazine or newspaper. This will usually enable the experienced advertiser to form a sufficiently accurate picture of the type of reader to which it appeals. Some publishers now prepare for advertisers carefully compiled statistics showing how many of their subscribers own automobiles, how many play golf, how many do this and how many do that.

Such statistics are helpful in suggesting purchasing power of subscribers.

11. *The flat rate.* Practically all magazine space is sold at the same price regardless of the amount of space used. This is known as a "flat rate." Many of the smaller newspapers also sell on flat rate; the larger newspapers, however, still have in many cases what are called "sliding scale rates." A sliding scale rate is based on the number of lines of space used by an advertiser during a year. The advertiser who uses only a thousand lines pays, perhaps, fifty per cent more per line than the advertiser who uses 20,000 lines. Nevertheless, the tendency among large as well as small papers is to adjust their schedules on the flat rate basis; most advertisers prefer this arrangement, and the advertising agencies are demanding it.

Nearly all agricultural publications sell space on the flat rate basis. Trade, technical and class publications are still inclined to the sliding scale rate, and in this field the rates vary more than in any other.

Some newspapers have two rates, charging one to national advertisers (known in the newspaper field as "foreign advertisers") and another to local or retail advertisers. In some cases the national rate is lower than the local rate, and in other cases it is higher.

12. *Preferred position.* It seems to be established that certain parts of a periodical publication are more desirable advertising media than others. The outside back cover, for instance, is considered a particularly desirable position—so desirable, indeed, that the back cover of the Ladies' Home Journal sells for $15,000 an issue, while the regular page rate is only $8,000. The inside cover

pages sell for $12,000 each. There is preferred position in newspapers as well as in magazines—top of column, for instance, next to reading matter. The constant cry for "position" is the bane of the newspaper publishers' existence. Most of them protect themselves by adding a charge, running up to twenty-five per cent of the regular space rates, when an advertiser specifies the particular position he wants his advertisement to occupy.

The desire to have advertisements appear next to reading matter is largely responsible for the present tendency to increase the size of the magazine page. Most publishers who have enlarged their pages, still keep the advertisements in the front and the back of their publications, but they have few pages carrying advertisements exclusively; usually there is a column of reading matter and two columns of advertisements on one of two facing pages.

13. *When to use preferred position.* In choosing an advertising medium the advertiser must consider the competition with other advertisements which his advertisements will meet. To get the maximum amount of attention, he must dominate. If all other posters near his are sixteen-sheet posters, he may get more attention by introducing an eight-sheet poster, but he will probably get most attention by using a twenty-four-sheet poster. If a sufficiently increased number of people will see an advertisement because it occupies unusually large space or because it occupies preferred position, the large space and the preferred position are worth the increased investment, to the extent that the advertiser can afford to pay for an increased number of readers, and to the extent that the proportionate increase in cost of space actually measures the increased attention value of the advertisement. Some attempt has been made by psychologists to establish general principles to guide the advertiser in the solution of this difficult problem, but the tests so far conducted are not conclusive enough for the average advertiser. Each advertiser must make his own experiments, finally standardizing on the space and position that his own experience, added to the experience of others, proves to be best adapted to serve his particular purposes.

ADVISORY 8

WEIGHING PRESTIGE

1. *The meaning of prestige.* In weighing the value of an advertising medium, the advertiser first considers its circulation—the unit cost of reaching each possible purchaser. The careful study of this problem involves all the things discussed in the last chapter. After weighing circulation, the advertiser next asks himself this question: What is the prestige of the medium? Prestige means influence. The prestige of an advertising medium is the influence it has on its readers. Its prestige is measured by the confidence of its advertisers. Prestige is important to the advertiser because the degree to which readers will be influenced by advertisements appearing in a medium is largely determined by their confidence in it. No two media have exactly the same prestige; the advertiser's problem is to pick out those media that will have the most influence on the particular class of people that he wishes to reach.

2. *Prestige of direct media.* The prestige of direct media varies in three ways. First, it varies with the kind of the medium. A sealed letter sent out under a two-cent stamp, for instance, ordinarily carries more prestige than an unsealed letter under one-cent postage. Second, the prestige of a direct medium varies with the quality of the medium. An attractive, clean-cut letterhead has more prestige than a slovenly, poorly arranged one. A good advertising specialty—a paper-knife, for instance, strong, durable, attractive—has more prestige than one that is badly constructed and obviously cheap. Third, every direct medium shares the prestige of the advertiser who uses it. A form letter from a well-known, highly respected business establishment has more prestige than an equally good letter from a house of which the recipient has never heard.

3. *Prestige of signs.* Many forms of signs at one time had little prestige. When posters were pasted chiefly on fences, dead walls and everything else except when kept off by a "Post No Bills" notice, many advertisers and many members of the public did not take posters very seriously. Now, however, the bill-posting business has been made a real business. Bill-boards are standardized media; they are placed where a known amount of traffic regularly passes; and the space they occupy is leased and paid for. Posters, too, have improved in character; the advertiser strives now for artistic attractiveness. Posters' art is gradually developing as a branch of art, as well as a branch of advertising. There is still some esthetic objection to all posters, but this attitude of a small minority is certainly not lessening the influence of billboards. Poster advertising has proved its value to many advertisers. Signs of all kinds are steadily gaining in prestige and in value as advertising media.

4. *How prestige works.* Mr. John Lee Mahin, in his book "Advertising—Selling the Consumer," gives an interesting illustration of the way in which prestige makes itself felt. He asks you to assume that you are on the mailing list of a bond house, and that you are also a regular reader of a morning paper, a monthly magazine and an illustrated weekly. One morning you receive from the bond house a circular describing a new issue of attractive investment bonds. It happens, that same day, that you see advertisements of those same bonds in your newspaper, your favorite magazine and your illustrated weekly. Assume that in all cases the advertisements are well prepared, and each one, regardless of the medium in which it appears, goes far toward influencing you favorably with respect to the bond issue. Which medium would have the greatest influence with you?

If your purchases from the bond house that sends you the circular have been profitable, the direct advertising of the circular would probably have the most prestige. If your experiences with that house, however, have been unpleasant—if you have been indifferently served, or if you have been dissatisfied with your purchases for any reason—the circular will have little influence. The circular would carry little prestige, also, if you had never heard of the house issuing it. In both these latter cases, an advertisement carrying the prestige of your favorite newspaper or magazine would probably be more influential than the circular.

If a bond house were to advertise in periodical media, and were also to send you a circular, the circular might influence you favorably, even if you had never heard of the advertiser before, because the advertisements in your favorite magazine and newspaper would give to the circular a prestige that it could not have if it stood alone.

5. *Factors in prestige.* The prestige of direct media and of signs cannot be measured by the application of any formula. Each advertiser must measure it by a study of local sentiment, by a study of his own past experiences and the experiences of others, and by a wise exercise of his own judgment. There is no formula, either, for weighing the prestige of periodicals; individual judgment here, as in the case of the two other kinds of media, must be largely relied on. Yet, in the case of periodicals, there are certain tangible factors to be used in the weighing process which are usually absent in measuring the prestige of direct media and signs.

Prestige is the result of character. A man's reputation is the world's estimate of his character, and reputation is based on habits. The same thing is true of a periodical. The advertiser can judge its prestige by considering its habits. These "habits" are usually termed policies, and they have to do with three different phases of the management of a publication:

1. The policies of the editorial department
2. The policies of the circulation department
3. The policies of the advertising department.

6. *Editorial policy.* The policies of the editorial department of any medium have much to do with measuring the degree to which advertisements appearing in that medium will influence its readers. Editorial policy largely determines the reader's attitude toward everything in the periodical. Someone has said: "The mission of an advertisement is threefold—to be seen, to be remembered and to be believed, and the greatest of these is to be believed." Unless a reader believes what he sees in the news columns he can scarcely be expected to have much faith in the advertisements. Accuracy of statement, a record for conservative understatement rather than habitual publication of mere rumors, and a proved desire to play fair with the public, build for a publication a body of readers who believe in it and in what it says. Such a publication has prestige of the first rank. The confidence bred by an editorial policy founded on a real affection for the truth is not confined to the news and editorial departments; it works for every advertiser who uses such a medium. The reader who believes in his favorite magazine or newspaper is very

likely to believe in the advertisements that appear in it. Editorial policy also helps the advertiser to determine what kind of people read a publication, as well as the length of time that the average reader may be expected to give to its perusal.

7. *Circulation policy.* The Audit Bureau of Circulations asks some pertinent questions in regard to how circulation is obtained, in an effort to find out what prestige the publication has in the minds of its readers. The first general question is: Have the readers all purchased the publication? Publications are asked to report the number of free copies circulated as well as the number of paid copies. They are asked to report the number of copies sold in bulk as well as those sold to individual subscribers. Publishers are asked how long subscribers are carried in arrears, and what proportion of their subscribers are in arrears.

In the case of a subscription publication the percentage of annual renewals is a guide to the number of people who consider the publication necessary. Voluntary renewals of subscriptions are valuable indications of prestige.

Newspapers are also asked to divide their circulation by editions, stating the hour each edition is published. Some advertisers believe that the time of day when a reader receives a publication is a measure of the degree of thoroness with which it is read. If a medium is only hastily perused, the reader's attention is not likely to be held very long by the advertisements appearing in it.

8. *Morning and evening papers.* Morning and evening papers are frequently in competition, and their publishers set up competing claims of superiority for their publications as advertising media. Some morning papers see no good in evening papers, and some evening papers see no good in morning papers. Each kind of publication has its partisans among advertisers. The controversy leads into a discussion of the habits of people in different localities—what proportion of the morning papers are read by men on their way to work and are little seen by women in the home, what proportion of the population spends its evenings at places of amusement instead of quietly at home in the company of the evening newspaper, and. a variety of similar considerations. The fact seems to be that neither morning nor evening papers, as a class, can claim superiority. Both have been proved to be good advertising media. In some communities, it is true, an evening paper is the recognized leader, while in others a morning paper leads as the better medium; but, where this is the case, the superiority seldom results from the fact that the

leader is an evening or a morning paper—usually it is due to other elements of prestige entirely independent of the time when the paper is issued.

9. *Sales and subscription magazines.* A sales magazine is one sold chiefly at news-stands or by newsboys. A subscription magazine is one sent chiefly to regular subscribers. Each, as an advertising medium, has its advocates. Those in favor of news-stand circulation say that when a reader takes the trouble to buy any particular issue of a magazine at a news-stand, it argues a real value which he attaches to that issue, and he is likely to read it carefully; while certain issues of a subscription magazine, coming periodically throughout the year, may be left unread or only hastily perused. The advocates of subscription magazines maintain that subscription circulation usually means home circulation; furthermore, a subscription to a magazine implies prestige—it means a definite desire for the publication on the part of the subscriber.

The truth probably lies in the fact that no periodical is a good or a bad advertising medium just because it has a news-stand circulation or because it has a regular circulation among subscribers. Here, as in the controversy between evening and morning papers, value as an advertising medium is chiefly determined by elements of prestige in the minds of readers, entirely independent of the ways in which, or the time at which, the publication is purchased. If a magazine is sold largely at news-stands, the advertiser wants to know where the stands are situated and the class of people who patronize them. The people who buy a publication are more important than the way in which they buy it.

10. *Advertising policy.* Editorial policy is important to the advertiser because it serves as a general guide to the kind of people who read a periodical and to the amount of influence the medium is likely to have with its readers. Circulation policy is important because it indicates the actual value placed on a medium by those who read it. Both editorial policy and circulation policy, therefore, are important aids in the advertiser's task of weighing prestige. But more important, perhaps, than either of these is the policy of the advertising department. An advertisement, like a man, is known by the company it keeps. An advertising policy that directs the acceptance of any advertisement offered to a periodical, is likely to put an advertiser in bad company. The prestige of a publication largely depends on the desire and ability of the publisher to publish only such advertisements as are honest and do, not offend the taste or morals of its readers. A publication is not a

public institution. It may accept or reject such advertisements as it pleases. The publication that makes no rejections is likely to have little prestige.

The movement toward the censoring of advertisements has two phases. One is the tendency, dictated either by policy or conviction, to exclude advertisements—
medical and tobacco advertisements, for example—that might offend some portion of the readers of a publication. The other is the tendency to protect readers against loss by excluding dishonest advertisements. Probably the first step in the campaign against dishonesty in advertising was to exclude those patent medicine advertisements that made exaggerated claims. In order to be sure that they are on the safe side, many periodicals now exclude all advertisements of patent medicines, regardless of their wording.

The second step in the campaign for honest advertising was the careful study of all advertisements submitted to a publication, to the end that the publisher might be certain his readers would not be defrauded or even misled by anything appearing in his advertising columns. This important movement has made tremendous strides. Only a few years ago almost any advertisement would be accepted by almost any publication. Today there are very few publications that do not exclude entirely certain classes of what they believe to be objectionable advertising, and which do not make some attempt to convince themselves of the honest purpose of every applicant for space. The extent to which this is done varies in different publications. Many publishers actually guarantee the truth of every word in every advertisement appearing in their columns.

11. *Typical advertising policies.* Farm journals in many cases have taken an advanced stand for honest advertising. A typical story is told of one farm paper that accepted in good faith the advertisement of a manufacturer of a new type of farm machinery. The manufacturer was entirely honest in his purpose; he believed his machine was meritorious and that he could make good all claims in his advertisements. The publisher investigated the business carefully, was convinced that it was sound and honest in every way, and accepted a one-time advertisement for which he was paid less than $300. Three of his readers bought the advertised machine at $750 each. Deliveries were not made when promised, and, when the machines did arrive, they did not come up to the claims of the advertisement. The publisher, when complaints reached him, immediately sent his check reimbursing each subscriber in full. Such high-minded concern for the welfare of readers

builds the strongest kind of prestige. One does not wonder that advertisers eagerly seek space in publications that take this advanced stand to protect their readers.

No particular class of publication is alone in the movement for honest advertising. As a body the general magazines led the way. Many years ago they began to "clean up" by excluding all false, fraudulent and otherwise objectionable advertisements. The anticipation was that this action would raise the tone of magazine publicity and attract a new and greater volume of advertising. The anticipation was realized. There is no question that the inauguration of this significant policy is responsible in large measure for the rapid and extraordinary development of advertising which followed it. As soon as the excellent results of the policy were perceived, the magazines hastened to take the further step of guaranteeing magazine readers against financial loss incurred from patronizing magazine advertisements. Virtually all general magazines now do this. A number of newspapers have put themselves on the same high plane. So have most of the agricultural press. The out-door display
interests, theater program publishers, street car advertising companies, and the technical and business publications are similarly "clean," though they do not guarantee against loss.

As illustrative of the policy adopted by many magazines we quote the following statement of censorship exercised by the Curtis Publishing Company with reference to advertisements which will be accepted for the Saturday Evening Post and the Ladies' Home Journal:

The Saturday Evening Post and the Ladies' Home Journal accept no advertisements

1. Of medical or curative agents of any kind
2. Of alcoholic beverages
3. Of subjects immorally suggestive
4. Of a nature unduly cheap or vulgar, or that is too unpleasant either in subject or treatment
5. Of a "blind" character—that is to say, advertising which in purpose and intent is obscure or misleading
6. Of "free" articles unless the article is actually free (a thing is not free if the reader is obliged to perform some service or buy some other article in order to obtain it)

7. Of a financial nature, if highly speculative
8. "Knocking" competitors

      The associates of one's advertisements are just as important indications of character as the associates of an individual. We repeat: The objects of an advertisement are three: to be seen, to be remembered, and to be believed, and the greatest of these is to be believed. One should prepare his advertisements and choose his media with this thought uppermost in mind.

ADVISORY 9

LETTERS AND DIRECT ADVERTISING

1. *Components of direct advertising.* All direct advertising thru the mail centers about the letter. In a broad sense any letter written to a customer or prospect for the purpose of obtaining business partakes of the nature of advertising. But this term is not often applied to general correspondence where each letter is personal; it is used to signify form letters reproduced by mechanical processes and sent to lists of persons together with the accompanying inclosures. It stands mid-way between the sales letter and general publicity. One is written for a particular person and sent to him directly, the other is addressed to all the persons of a group whom it reaches indirectly. Mail advertising while general in its appeal to all the persons in a group is sent to them directly as individuals.

2. *Advantages of mail campaigns.* Direct advertising thru the mail, as compared with the more indirect methods of advertising, has several strong points in its favor. Among these may be mentioned the advertiser's ability (1) to limit the expense of his campaign; (2) to guard trade information; (3) to concentrate his advertising upon a particular community or a particular class of people; (4) to time the reading of the advertisement; and (5) to make enclosures of samples or return envelops that encourage the prospect to order on the spot.

Mail advertising permits the expenditure of small or large sums of money as conditions may dictate. The sum spent for sending out a series of letters is determined mostly by the length of the manager's mailing list. In magazine advertising, on the other hand, the cost comes in large units. To an inadequately financed business, this consideration is especially important; tho even a successful and amply financed business must select its advertising media according to the limits set by its advertising appropriation.

The advertiser may choose mail advertising as the best means of controlling trade information. Special price appeals may be made thru this medium with less danger of incurring the ire of competitors. Patents, new types of machines, new patterns in fabrics—the particulars of these must, of course, be disclosed in order to sell the product; yet the advertiser may wish to confide his plans only to a limited number of prospective buyers. The advantages of an "underground" campaign are well appreciated by practical advertisers.

An advertisement in a dental magazine might seem sure to reach a definite and homogeneous class of people. Nevertheless, a mailing list of the dentists graduated from the University of Illinois would enable the advertiser to reach a group within a group.

An advertising letter to such an inner group may be composed so as to make an especially strong appeal. In the same way a thorough test may be made of a particular locality by directing mail matter to all the known prospects, and adapting what is sent to special local needs.

Mail advertising permits the advertiser to time the reading of the advertisement more exactly. If the prospect is a dealer, he will probably open the letter at his desk. If the letter contains a stamped and addressed inclosure, the conditions are good for getting an immediate response. An advertisement in the dealer's trade magazine, on the other hand, may fall under his eye on the car home, or at some other time when active response is impossible. Again printed advertisements only receive a limited degree of attention, so that a full description of a product in a "printed advertisement" would be impracticable, the more so since the description would probably be in fine print.

3. *The uses of direct advertising.* Direct advertising may be used to get orders directly or it may be employed for other purposes. It may be used to supplement the work of traveling salesmen. It is often used to precede the introduction of a new specialty or a new policy, which assures the salesman when he calls that the prospect is at least partially informed in regard to the organization and product which he represents. The form letter is used also to introduce a new salesman, and thus often prepares a welcome for him when he calls.

It is becoming more and more difficult for a salesman to work advantageously without active support from the house which he represents. Direct advertising provides a means by which the salesman's statements are authoritatively supported over the signature of one of the officials of his company.

A certain sales manager estimates that his firm loses $8,500 a year thru calls by his salesmen upon buyers who are absent from their offices at the time of the call. He could save that loss if he could devise an appointment system that would insure that the buyer would be on hand when the salesman calls. Direct advertising may help in such a case. Even though it fails to insure an appointment in every instance, it may indicate whether or not it is worth while for the salesman to go to great trouble to make an appointment with a particular prospect.

The visit of a salesman is a large expense, and there are many dealers to see and few salesmen to see them. By using letters at frequent intervals, to supplement the calls of salesmen, the manufacturer or jobber is enabled to keep closely in touch with his distributors and at the same time out down expense.

4. *Compiling the mailing list.* The success of a mail campaign depends primarily upon the mailing list. Bad advertising matter sent to a live list is no doubt partly wasted, but good advertising sent to a bad list is yet more futile.

The first step in compiling a mailing list is to determine what class of people are most likely to buy the goods offered. Certain broad classifications may be quickly determined; for example, those based on sex, on occupation, on income, or on foreign extraction.

Business and professional men are said to be liberal buyers of certain commodities, while bankers and farmers are conservative buyers.
The selection of the sources of mailing list names is seldom difficult. The following outline is suggestive of the many mines of information for the wide-awake advertiser.

I.   Directories
    a. Local
       i. City
      ii. Telephone
     iii. Social registers, "blue books," etc.

b. Sectional and national
  i. Rating books
  ii. Trade directories
II. Government records
  a. Local
    i. City and county tax lists
    ii. Building permits
    iii. License and marriage records
    iv. Registration lists
  b. State
    i. Secretary of State's records (automobile licenses, for example)
    ii. Labor reports
  c. National
    i. Income tax limits
    ii. Consular reports
    iii. Departmental publications (notably, reports of the Bureau of Foreign and Domestic Commerce)
III. Organizations
  a. Business (Commercial clubs)
  b. General
    i. Fraternal
    ii. Social
    iii. Labor
IV. Press clippings (press clippings may be collected about any subject affecting the advertiser's interests; e.g., names of advertisers, society notes, fires, births, marriages, deaths, transfers of real estate, etc.)
V. Advertising (study of advertisements in all kinds of periodicals yields valuable names for a mailing list)
VI. Miscellaneous
  a. Employees of business houses
  b. Lists exchanged with other advertisers .
  c. Listing companies
  d. Addressing companies
  e. Special investigations, full or part time
  f. Reports of salesmen
  g. Customers
  h. Banks
  i. Dealers

    j. Advertising departments of periodicals

    k. Accounts in sales ledger

One of the quickest ways to construct a live mailing list of general consumers is to offer something at a reduced price in a magazine, newspaper, or other periodical medium. One of the great mail-order houses obtained its first mailing list from publishing advertisements offering thirty pounds of sugar for a dollar. Within a few days the company had the names of thousands of people who had demonstrated their willingness to buy direct by mail when exceptional value is offered. Among other ingenious schemes of this sort are prize offers and voting contests.

Valuable mailing lists may be purchased on very short notice from listing agencies and addressing companies. The price of these lists varies with the difficulty of compiling them and ranges from one cent to as high as fifty cents a name. Reputable, listing agencies usually guarantee their lists to be from 95 to 98 per cent accurate, according to the nature of the list; and they refund for all "dead letters." In buying "names" it is well to stipulate that letters returned because of wrong or insufficient address shall call for a refund.

5. *Getting a correct list*. In establishing a list for mailing purposes it pays to spend thought and care to get it correct. One defect in lists compiled from directories is that commonly only the first and last name are given in full; while the middle name is indicated by initials. The John H. Smith of the directory may sign his name in any of various ways. He may prefer to he addressed as "J. H. Smith," or "John Hepburn Smith," or possibly "J. Hepburn Smith." He may also prefer to be addressed with whatever titular degree or other designation he is accustomed to.

The subject of "right names" was investigated by a well-known publishing company. By comparative tests the company found that a list made up of names as customarily signed achieved results 14 2/3 per cent better than a list copied from a directory.

Oftentimes names and addresses of the same persons are obtainable from different sources and one can be used to check the other.

The nature of the business will to a great extent determine whether other information besides name and address is desirable. In some retail businesses where it is expected to serve the same customer many times the facts collected by the advertiser concerning birthday dates, political and religious affiliations, size of family and similar matters are numerous.

6. *Keeping lists up-to-date*. When it is expected to use the lists over and over again, they require continual care. A list, once compiled, never stays put. A good mailing list is the product of a constant evolution. People move away, or die, or change their occupations and the mailing list must be revised or scrapped. The rate of depreciation to which a particular list is subject is determined naturally by the nature of the list. A list of farmers who own their own farms may not vary one per cent a year. At the other extreme, a list of salesmen of cheap specialties may have to be revised every month.

One man's "mailing-list creed" reads as follows: "Every possible customer who is not on my list represents a leak in my future profits: every man on my list who is not a possible customer represents a leak in present expenses." Constant revising and refining is expensive, but habitual neglect is more expensive.

A local merchant has, in the new editions of local directories, a fairly dependable source from which to revise his list. A national advertiser, however, having on his lists names scattered over small towns and rural districts, may not always find directories available. In such a case, perhaps the best method of checking is to send a copy of the list for each town to the postmaster with the request that he cross off the names of all who have left the town. If the postmaster is tactfully approached he may usually be induced to perform this service, but the law forbids his adding new names to the list.

7. *Filing the mailing cards*. The necessity of filing cards for mailing lists is patent when we consider the frequency of corrections, of removals, of additions, and of new classifications, especially those new classifications necessary when a prospect has been appealed to or when he has responded to the mail campaign. A certain national concern divides its cards into fifteen distinct classes. Its first three classifications—manufacturers, wholesalers and retailers—are filed together alphabetically, the three classes being distinguished by metallic index tabs. Using cards of different colors is another method of subdividing a file and may be used in coordination with the index tabs. The practice of using a single subdivided file is especially commendable where all cards are periodically checked from directories, rating books, or other alphabetical sources; but it is always commendable in that it

saves time in searching for a card. The use of several files usually necessitates a great deal of extra work in duplicating cards for cross filing.

8. *Sales by mail*. The components of any mail-selling campaign are usually a series of letters, often with appropriate enclosures. A single letter does not make a campaign. There must be a suitable follow up or the initial effort is largely wasted.

Whether the letters should be composed for climactic effect, or whether the strongest appeal should be made in the first letter, is an important problem in planning the series. A cardinal principle in direct mail advertising, however, is that each mailing should be sufficient in itself to convince the prospect and induce him to act without awaiting subsequent mailings. Even where the climactic plan is not followed, the time element in the follow-ups deserves attention. The old rule that follow-ups should be sent ten days apart is greater in simplicity than in sales value. In timing follow-ups, importance again attaches to the class of prospects appealed to. A business man answers letters the day they arrive: the farmer or laborer ordinarily is not so prompt.

9. *Raking the list*. Where an expensive booklet is used to describe the goods, it is not advisable to send out the booklet promiscuously to a large list. Instead, a strong appeal should be sent out inviting all interested in securing the booklet to mail an enclosed card. Some companies having only inexpensive booklets have found by investigation that though more replies come when stamped envelopes are enclosed, the increase of returns may not warrant the additional expense.

Again, to arouse interest in a proposition a series of "mailing pieces" may be sent to a list of names. The mailing pieces consist of cards or circulars designed in striking and elaborate style, each presenting one definite point about the product or its use. In each of them a drive is made for a reply from the prospect. When the reply comes, the mailing of the pieces is of course discontinued. At this point the expensive catalog is sent, or the salesman makes a call.

10. *The trial campaigns*. The list compiled, the letters prepared, and all details of posting decided, it may prove profitable to test the campaign on a representative group of prospects before driving forward on a large scale. An advertiser having a list of, say, 20,000 names may take the first 500 in alphabetical order, and mail his letters to them, keeping careful records of the returns. He may be reasonably

certain that his percentage of replies will be about the same from the whole 20,000 as they were from the first 500.

The following figures are from an actual test of a direct-by-mail campaign to secure subscriptions to a publication. The prospects were all bankers. No follow-ups were used. The advertiser established as his minimum twenty orders a thousand; and if a letter did not "pull" to that extent, he saved himself the expense of sending it to the entire list. The percentage returns from the tests and from the actual mailings were found to be nearly the same.

BANKERS' TESTS

Material mailed	No. of pieces mailed	Tests total orders received	No. per 1,000	No. of pieces mailed	Total orders received	No. per 1,000
A2	500	5	10			1000
B1	500	6	12			
C1	500	4	8			
E	500	7	14			
F1	500	24	36	16,511	589	35
F2	1000	30	30	21,790	643	29.5
G	500	12	24	16,039	390	24
H	500	12	24	6,810	145	
I	500	12		12,154	336	25

11. *Tests of follow-up series.* A trial campaign to establish the proper number of letters in a series of follow-ups may require so much time as to be impossible. The advertiser may be compelled to decide from judgment rather than from experiment. He knows that in the first part of the series the succession of appeals will operate to his favor but that a "diminishing return" will operate against him somewhere in the latter part of the series. Just where in the series will one additional letter be unprofitable? The remainder of this chapter is devoted to precisely this question.

Following is a record of seventeen follow-up letters which were sent at weekly intervals to 2,300 dealers in twelve eastern states to induce them to carry the Moneybak Taffeta Selvage Silks, made by the New York Silk Manufacturing Company. The entire campaign cost $1,554.

Letter No.	Requests for samples	Orders from new accounts
1	1	0
2	5	5
3	4	5
4	3	7
5	8	10
6	3	7
7	6	6
8	6	14
9	2	5
10	5	7
11	16	7
12	7	9
13	7	8
14	4	12
15	3	3
16	3	6
17	10	33

Eleven of these letters, one to eleven inclusive, were used on another list of 4,800 dealers in the remaining state of the country, with the results shown in the following table:

Letter No.	Requests for samples	Orders from new accounts
1	13	3
2	0	19
3	5	9
4	3	12
5	8	12
6	3	12
7	9	7
8	8	22
9	2	20
10	3	6
11	0	4

12. *Taking the average of a series.* Another interesting record shows the returns from a series of six letters sent out by an advertising specialist who planned to make a six months' campaign pay on the basis of the net profit from new accounts.

Letter No.	Per cent of replies	Per cent of new accounts	Net profit on new accounts	Cost of campaign
1	12/3 of 1%	0	0	$85
2	2%	1/6 of 1%	$43	85
3	1/6 of 1%	0	0	85
4	1 1/3%	2/3 of 1%	2,570	85
5	3%	2/3 of 1%	427	85
6	7%	3%	2,000	85
Average	2 1/3%	2/3%	Total $5,040	$510

If this advertiser had stopped at the end of the third letter, as some might think he would have been justified in doing, he would have nothing but a new loss of $212 to show for his efforts. By continuing throughout the series, he was able to obtain new accounts on he received a net profit of about ten times the cost of the campaign.

REVIEW

- If it costs less to send a letter to a prospect than to se salesman, why send a salesman at all?
- What sources of names for a mailing list could be used in business? your
- Could letters be used to facilitate the work of salesmen in you business? If not, why not?
- Why must mailing lists be revised?
- Devise a system for handling the mailing cards after the mail campaign begins.
- How many the effectiveness of sales letters he tested? Why?

ADVISORY 10

SAMPLING

1. *Extent of sampling.* Sampling has been largely responsible for the success of many standard products. It is one of the oldest kinds of advertising and, when properly used, one of the best. Little has been written about it, however, and few records of sampling results have been. published. Probably there is no other branch of advertising on which there is so little available data as on the subject of sampling. The average advertiser knows that there are many forms of sampling, and he realizes that many deterrent things have been put on the market with the aid of sampling. He seldom knows all the ways in which sampling may be used, however, nor has he a clear conception of the widely varying commodities that are susceptible to this particular form of direct advertising.

In this chapter our purpose is to list the chief ways in which products are sampled, and to indicate the possibilities of sampling by naming actual articles that have been introduced by the various methods named. First, we are to consider typical methods of sampling direct by the manufacturer, and then various methods of using the dealer to get samples to consumers.

2. *General classes of sampling.* Sampling is or several kinds; the more important, which explain themselves, follow:

1. Putting on trial—the plan adopted in selling, talking machines, adding machines and type. writers.
2. Demonstrating in stores or at fairs—where the consumer is allowed to taste the food product or to try the use of the product for himself.

3. The most common form of sampling—the distributing of packages of the product for the ultimate consumer to use, cook or otherwise demonstrate to his or her own satisfaction.

3. ***Sampling through distribution by other manufacturers*** Many original methods of sampling have been discovered by clever merchandising men. One of the most successful is that of distributing samples thru other manufacturers. For several years, if you purchased any make of a revolver, you found in the case a neat and attractive sample of Three-In-One Oil. These samples were furnished to the revolver manufacturers without charge, and the revolver manufacturers were glad to distribute the samples in this way, believing that in so doing they were rendering a service to their customers.

4. ***House-to-house sampling***. The oldest method of sampling is to distribute packages from house to house. All sorts of things have been sampled in this way. An ice company in Kentucky once filled every ice-box in the town with a large-size sample of its goods. More often, however, house-to-house sampling is used for food products, washing preparations and other things that cost little and are used by everyone. Some food manufacturers re-sample a territory every two or three years. This costs much money, but in many cases it has proved profitable.

The success of house-to-house sampling depends largely on the care used by the sampling crew. Each package must get inside the door, because packages left outside are often collected by boys who follow the crew. It is argued, probably with justice, that the housewife who might not take the trouble to go to a store to exchange a coupon for a sample will use a sample if it is left at her home. House-to-house sampling is undoubtedly the most expensive kind of sampling; yet it seems to be the most successful in cities of medium size.

5. ***Sampling in public places***. One of the sampling methods used in distributing Wrigley's gums was sampling in theaters. A perfume manufacturer once arranged with a theater manager to attach a small sample vial of a new brand of perfume to every theater program distributed. The theater is a place where people can be reached in groups.

In cities with a population of a million or over, it is often found advisable to substitute sampling in public places for the house-to-house method. In New

York City food manufacturers often place sampling distributors at the elevated and subway stations at the time of the evening rush.

6. *Sampling where representative groups are congregated*. G. Washington Coffee was first introduced in Atlantic City, and was sampled there for several months during the summer convention season. The manufacturers found, as they expected, that from this sampling a demand for the coffee was soon created in many parts of the country. The Durham Duplex Razor was also sampled at Atlantic City, when a large national convention was held there. Everyone who attended the convention was given a full-size razor with a handle made of papier maché and carrying one blade only. As most safety razor manufacturers make their profit on the sale of the blades, in order to use the razor more than a few times the recipient was compelled to buy blades from his local distributor. Colgate & Company does extensive sampling of its different products at the large and more representative conventions.

The cigarette and tobacco companies have practiced public sampling on a scale far more extensive than any other class of advertisers.

7. *Demonstrating in consumers' homes*. Various brands of flour have been pushed in new territories by house-to-house canvassers who call on the housewives, explain the merits of the flour and give a cook-book or an order for flour, to be filled by the purchaser's own grocer. Products demonstrated in this way are usually sold at the full retail price the canvassers. Twenty Mule Team Borax and many kinds of baking powder have been introduced in this manner. It may be argued that this is merely direct-to-consumer selling, and not sampling at all. It is purely a form of advertising, because the method of sale is too expensive to be continued after the introductory period, and it has more in common with sampling than with any other kind of advertising.

8. *Lectures and sampling*. Some manufacturers employ lecturers and demonstrators to appear before women's clubs, schools of home economics and other groups of women, to explain their products, and incidentally, to distribute samples to the people present. Aluminum kitchen utensils have often been sampled in this way. Generally, however, the names of the people present at the lecture are taken in order that each person may be followed up by mail.

9. *Sampling in restaurants*. Some food manufacturers furnish free to all the leading restaurants in a city a sufficient amount of their products for one or two days' supply, and then advertise in the newspapers and in other ways the particular days at which these foods may be found on the menus of the restaurants. This was the plan used in introducing Cream of Rice in Chicago. Uneeda Biscuit was sampled at the Inside Inn at the St. Louis World's Fair in a similar manner.

10. *Sampling influential groups*. Some manufacturers find they can make no progress without the assistance of certain influential groups, such as doctors and dentists. These manufacturers provide for systematic sampling to those they wish to influence. Tooth powders and pastes, for example, are largely sampled in this way. National distribution has often been obtained practically by means of this kind of advertising alone. The entire effort is centered on getting the good-will of dentists, for instance, who frequently distribute to their patients the free samples sent to them for this purpose, and who, it is hoped will recommend the use of the sampled preparations.

11. *Sampling direct by mail*. Many manufacturers obtain lists of the most influential people in each community and send them samples of their products, accompanied by letters explaining the use of the goods. That is usually done after obtaining lists from dealers; some manufacturers, however, find it advisable to make up their own lists. Pluto Water has been introduced in this way in many territories. The Loose Wiles Biscuit Company has also used this plan in introducing many of its products.

A variation of this scheme is to send samples only when they are asked for. The Horlick's Malted Milk Company sends letters to special lists of prospects, with each letter inclosing a post-card for the prospect to use in asking for a sample if he is interested enough to give it a trial. This method of sampling eliminates waste, and is therefore preferred by many advertisers. Consumers are sometimes used in compiling lists of people to whom samples are to be sent. For many years each package of Kolynos tooth paste has carried an addressed post-card for the purchaser to use in sending to the manufacturer the names of friends who might be interested in the product. Sometimes a manufacturer makes a small gift to customers who cooperate with him in this way.

12. *Sampling at factory "house warmings."* When a manufacturer builds a new factory or establishes a new branch office or warehouse, if his product is of the

sort than can be sampled, he often invites the public to a "house warming," and distributes samples to all who attend.

13. *Sampling by using premiums*. Premiums are given for the return of wrappers and coupons from many kinds of goods. When a product carries premiums, it is common practice for a canvasser to go from house to house, explaining the goods, showing the premium—a set of silverware, perhaps—and telling the housewife that the premium will be given free if she collects a certain number of wrappers or coupons from the manufacturer's products. To enable her to start collecting, the canvasser may give her a free sample wrapper or a complete sample of the goods, or he may give her a sample on condition that she purchases more of the goods from him or from her dealer. One soap manufacturer reports that this is the most successful sampling scheme he has ever used.

14. *Sampling thru dealers*. The sampling methods thus far described are available to all manufacturers, whether they market their goods thru dealers or not. The manufacturer who sells thru dealers, however, has access to many other kinds of sampling. Dealers who know that a manufacturer will treat them fairly, who believe in his product, and who are satisfied with the profit they derive from its sale, are often willing to help the manufacturer distribute samples of the product among their customers for the purpose of increasing its sales. There are several common ways of sampling with the cooperation of dealers.

15. *Sampling with coupons*. Coupons are used in many ways in the distribution of samples. One frequently used plan is to distribute coupons from house to house or by mail, the coupons to be exchangeable for full-size samples at any store or at certain stores listed on the coupon. This is, in effect, house-to-house sampling, but with most of the waste eliminated. Of course, the manufacturer who uses this method runs the risk of failing to reach many desirable possible customers who will not go to the trouble of turning in a coupon to their grocer in exchange for a free sample, although they might use samples if the samples were left at their doors.

Another method of using coupons is to publish them in newspapers, instead of distributing them from house to house. A coupon, clipped from the paper and handed to a dealer, entitles a person to a sample of the goods. Sometimes there are no strings whatever to the offer; at other times the advertisement specifies that only one sample will be given to an individual or to a family. In still other cases a sample is given for a coupon only if a purchase of the manufacturer's goods is made at the same time; in other words, a coupon and five cents will purchase two five-cent cakes of soap.

Coupons for a new product are sometimes packed with older products of a manufacturer. The purchaser of the older product finds a coupon in it calling for a sample of a new line. He either sends the coupon direct to the manufacturer or, more often, exchanges it for a sample at a dealer's.

16. *Samples free with purchases*. Instead of requiring the possible customer to present a coupon, some manufacturers authorize dealers to give a sample of a new product to every purchaser of the manufacturer's older goods. For instance, when Violeta Soap was introduced in certain territories grocers were authorized to give away three cakes of the new soap with every twenty-five-cent purchase of any of Armour's other products. Sometimes the offer is a sample free with any purchase, regardless of the kind or value of the goods bought. When Air-Line Honey was introduced in Chicago, the distributers proclaimed an "Air Line Day," when a free sample of the honey was given to every purchaser in every grocery store that handled the goods. Some dealers now advertise "Sampling Days," at which times they give away samples of various kinds. Many advertisers, however, feel that such wholesale distribution is not profitable.

17. *Sampling in delivery packages*. Full size packages of Shredded Wheat have at various times been distributed to dealers, who were asked to include one of the samples in every assortment of goods delivered during a certain period. Some manufacturers find that grocers will not take the time to distribute their samples in this way; in such cases the manufacturer often stations his own men in the large stores to put samples in the delivery packages for the grocer.

18. *Sending samples with other goods*. Many manufacturers, instead of trying to sample systematically among a dealer's customers, simply send the dealer a few samples in the hope that he will distribute them where they will do the most good. When Wrigley's Doublemint gum was introduced, samples of it were sent with filled orders for the older Spearmint brand. Several sample bottles of Dioxogen were formerly shipped with each dealer's first order of the regular size packages. This is a good plan when the manufacturer can be reasonably sure that the dealer will really give the samples to purchasers.

19. *Sampling at demonstrations*. A favorite method of sampling is in connection with demonstrations. Manufacturers of food products and toilet preparations often obtain permission to establish demonstration booths in the stores of dealers who handle the goods to be demonstrated. Here visitors not only actually try the goods, but they are also given samples to take home with them. Crystal Domino Sugar was introduced in this way.

Occasionally manufacturers have thought it best to establish demonstration and sampling booths in stores that do not handle the goods displayed at the booths. Food products, for instance, are sometimes introduced thru demonstration booths in department stores that do not have grocery departments. This plan is followed because of the large number of people that visit department stores, and in the belief that this method of distributing will result in the goodwill of small grocers, who might possibly be antagonized by the active work of a manufacturer in the grocery department of one of their large competitors.

20. *Compensation to cooperating dealers*. A plan for distributing samples thru dealers is always met at the outset by the knowledge that many dealers may not be willing to cooperate. Ordinarily when a dealer is asked merely to distribute small-size samples to his customers, he does not seriously object, although even in this case some dealers refuse. They may say that they have no time to distribute samples for a manufacturer or they may believe that the distribution of a considerable number of small-size samples will hurt the sale of full-size packages of the goods. This latter objection would not be valid if the samples were distributed only to non-users of the sampled product; but unless care is taken to see that only this class of people receive the samples, possibly the dealer's sales do suffer.

The chief objection of dealers to the distribution of samples arises when full-size packages of the prod, not are given away. The various coupon methods of sampling, for example, usually provide for free distribution of regular sizes of the goods. The dealer says that every regular-size package given away means just one less package sold. Obviously, this position is not always logical. If a non-user gets the sample, he may become a regular user. But, except in the case of new articles, no effective way has been devised to insure free samples going only to nonusers. Many manufacturers get around this difficulty by paying the dealer the full retail price for all samples distributed at his store. For example, if a coupon is left with a housewife, and she takes it to her grocer, receiving in exchange a cake of soap that ordinarily sells for five cents, the manufacturer redeems the coupon for five cents, thus not only paying the grocer what the soap cost him, but also giving him the same profit on the transaction that he would have if he sold the soap instead of giving it away. In demonstrations carried on in stores it is customary for the manufacturer who is sampling his goods, if he uses full-size packages, to buy out of the dealer's stock at regular retail prices the goods that he needs for sampling. There are many variations in the plan of paying dealers to cooperate in the distribution of samples. The methods that have been described, however, are suggestive of the principles. It may be stated as a general rule that some plan of compensating dealers is almost necessary if their cooperation is expected in the giving away of samples to consumers.

REVIEW
- Judging from the classification of sampling made in the early. part of the chapter, what kinds of commodities do you consider lend themselves most readily to sampling?
- Which do not?
- For example, would you sample clothing, china ware, silverware, fruit?
- Could sampling be used in your business? If so, in what form?
- Does sampling thru dealers have any advantages over sampling direct to consumers? What obstacles have to be met in sampling thru dealers?
- What are the advantages and disadvantages of sampling by means of coupons?

ADVISORY 11

HOW PERIODICALS ARE USED

1. *Place of periodicals in the campaign.* In previous chapters we have listed the various kinds of periodical media and have briefly shown how they are related to the other media that are available for the carrying of the advertiser's message. In this chapter we are to consider more in detail the way in which periodicals are used. The periodical is the great advertising medium. To many people the word advertising suggests only advertising in newspapers, magazines and other publications. This is too narrow a conception of advertising. Direct media and signs are just as legitimate and just as important aids in a campaign as are the various kinds of periodicals. For some commodities, direct media or signs may be the only possible methods of reaching the buying public. For others, periodical advertising alone may be unable to accomplish the desired result.

2. *Kinds of newspaper advertising.* First in volume of advertising carried by periodicals are the newspapers. The newspaper is used by more advertisers, reaches more people, and reaches them more often than any other advertising medium. Newspaper advertising is generally divided into three classes:
   1. Local retail advertising
   2. Classified advertising
   3. Foreign advertising

   a. Local retail advertising. Most newspaper advertising belongs in the first two classes. There are something over three-quarters of a million retail stores in the United States. Many of them do little or no advertising. The larger ones and the successful ones, however, are usually persistent advertisers, and it is their publicity that makes the average newspaper possible. The advantages of newspaper advertising for retail stores no longer need to be argued. The right kind of newspaper advertising pays; thousands and thousands of stores the country over have proved it. If a store is a good store, if it sells good goods and gives good service, only one thing more is essential to success-that the public shall know about the store and what it has to offer. Ordinarily the best and cheapest way to tell the public is thru the newspaper.

b. Classified advertising. Small advertisements, usually set in small type, of the sort ordinarily known as "Want Ads," are known as classified advertising. These advertisements are usually local in character positions wanted, positions to be tilled, local business opportunities, articles lost and found, etc. Some national advertisers, however, have used classified advertisements effectively. The fact that the "Want Ad" columns are carefully read by certain groups of people results in a sure, even if not always a large audience for the manufacturer who puts his advertising message in those columns.

c. Foreign advertising in a newspaper is ordinarily the advertising of manufacturers whose plants are located elsewhere than in the city in which the news, paper is published. When modern advertising began to develop, the newspapers were practically the only available media for a national campaign then came the magazines, and for a while the news. papers were less used by national advertisers. Of late years, however, manufacturers have more and more used newspapers in connection with magazines and other forms of advertising, and some have used newspapers exclusively. Newspapers offer to the national advertiser an effective method of concentrating a sales appeal in a desirable territory, either at the beginning of a campaign or after the campaign has started and weaknesses have developed in certain localities.

3. *How newspapers are used by manufactures*. In selling products of a certain sort, it is often good policy not to attempt to cover the whole country at the start, but to "open up" one jobbing center at a time.

Newspaper advertising may be employed successfully in such a case. The local newspaper campaigns will probably be supported by sampling and the use of other advertising media. Grocery specialties are ordinarily introduced in this way. Later part of the advertising appropriation may be spent in the magazines. These advertisers, however, keep close track of the distribution and sale of their products, and whenever they find a city in which per capita consumption is below normal, a concentrated newspaper campaign is often undertaken in order to increase sales locally. Although some national advertisers use newspapers the year around, most of the "foreign" newspaper advertising appears only for limited periods. The Coca-Cola Company, for example, uses newspapers chiefly when there are conventions or unusual gatherings in a certain city, and it is desirable to reach those in attendance in an intensive way. Other advertisers cultivate a local field by using newspaper advertisements for a period of a month, two months, half a year or longer.

4. *Size of newspaper advertisements*. The standard newspaper page consists of seven columns of thirteen pica ems (2 1/8 inches) in width, and from twenty to twenty-two, inches in depth. In the larger cities the eight column newspaper is being adopted very rapidly. Very few campaigns will warrant the use of an entire page for each advertisement. Some advertisers make all their newspaper advertisements the same size.

The question of the number of insertions and the size of space is one of the most difficult ones in all advertising. The larger sizes of space command the greater attention. A newspaper is issued 365 days in a year. The question is, "How often do I need to advertise and how small can my space be in order to get the attention I desire?" The problem can only be answered by constant tests. The first step is to decide upon a uniform proportion. The smallest advertisement with pleasing proportions is the one column 50 line advertisement; it is approximately 3 1/2 inches deep. The two column advertisement of this same proportion is practically 7 inches deep and totals 200 lines. The following table shows the different sizes of advertisements which may be made from this proportion:

Columns in width	Depth in lines	Depth in inches (approximately)	Total number of lines
1	50	3 $\frac{1}{2}$	50
2	100	7	200
3	150	10 $\frac{1}{2}$	450
4	200	14	800
5	250	18 $\frac{1}{2}$	1250
6	300	21 $\frac{1}{2}$	1800

The Sims Cereal Company has a certain limited appropriation which is based upon the expected sales in any particular city. It has experimented with the smallest size advertisement and finds, that in order to get returns, it must advertise at least once a week. It finds that the returns drop in a greater proportion to the investment if it advertises only once every two weeks and that they do not increase in proportion to the investment if it advertises two, three, four, five or six times a week. It has found the particular day of the week in which it is most profitable to advertise and has established once a week as the minimum number of insertions. As the territory produces business, it increases the size of space until all 52 advertisements in its year's campaign are of the 200 line size. Then it commences with the 450 line size until all 52 advertisements are of that size in that city and so proceeds to increase the size of space on the minimum number of insertions advisable until it has reached the page unit. By increasing its size of advertisement on the same proportion, the expense of making drawings of different shapes is saved, it is possible to achieve uniformity in mechanical layout and the reader recognizes the advertisements as having grown in size but not having changed in form. The reader is hardly conscious of any variation in the frequency of the appearances of an advertisement, but he is mightily impressed by increase in size.

5. *Amount of space used in newspapers*. Some national advertising campaigns in newspapers call for insertions every day, some three times a week, some twice a week, some once a week and some at other intervals. The advertiser must be careful in choosing his days and the frequency of insertion.

The amount of space one can afford to use in the newspaper, the amount of space in each paper to be used in order to secure the desired attention, the length of the campaign, and the frequency of insertions all depend on the nature of the product advertised, the habits of possible customers in relation to the newspaper, and the size, display and frequency of other advertising in the same newspaper.

6. *Use of magazines*. The magazine generally is recognized as the great national medium. It is set to advertise products which have a national distribution or national sales possibilities. It is employed for a great number of different kinds of goods. One kind of magazine advertising is that which has for its purpose the sending of consumers to retail stores to buy the products of advertising manufacturers. Perhaps the majority of magazine advertisements are of this sort. Another large group is composed of the advertisements of manufacturers and dealers who do business by mail. Advertisements in this class may be intended either to induce immediate mail orders, or they may have for their purpose the

eliciting of inquiries from possible purchasers, which are followed up by the advertiser and later develop into sales. Inquiries from readers are the primary object, too, of some advertisers whose goods are sold thru dealers; the inquiries are turned over to local dealers after being obtained thru magazine advertising. Other inquiries obtained thru advertising are turned over to the advertiser's salesmen to be developed into sales if possible.

Some magazine advertising has for its chief purpose the obtaining of distribution. The word distribution is arbitrarily used by advertisers to refer to the handling of goods by retailers. A manufacturer who is advertising "to get distribution" is trying to induce retailers to handle his product. After distribution. is obtained, magazine advertising may be used to increase the good-will and cooperation of dealers.

A few retailers advertise in magazines ordinarily, though, only when they want mail orders, or when a chain of stores has retail establishments in many cities. The S. S. Kresge Company having 170 retail stores in different parts of the United States uses magazines to advertise its services.

To catalog all the possible uses of magazine advertising would be to state the purposes of the majority of all the national advertising campaigns. There are hundreds of things that can be done with media of large circulation reaching readers all over the country. The magazine more than any other medium, perhaps, has made it possible for the manufacturer to establish a sure market for his goods-to put them in packages, trade-mark them, and then to tell the consuming public about them in such a forceful, attractive way that a steady demand for them is gradually built up. Magazine advertising has been an exceedingly effective tool in bringing the manufacturer and his market close together, in educating the public with respect to new things, in teaching values, and in standardizing the use of hundreds of time and labor-saving devices all over the country.

One of the most extensive magazine campaigns ever conducted was that for the sale of the eleventh edition of the Encyclopedia Britannica. Several pages, sometimes with inserts, were used in each issue of a large list of national magazines. The purpose of the campaign was twofold. First, to tell the .pub lie about the encyclopedia and to create interest in it. second, to obtain 1nquiries, which were turned over to salesmen in the field. There was little expectation that direct mail orders would result in sufficient num. her to pay for the advertising. A few orders came direct by mail; most of the business, however, was obtained thru salesmen. The advertising was a tremendous help to the salesmen in two ways. The inquiries, of course, gave the salesmen direct "leads" in many cases. A man who has taken the trouble to inquire about something that is advertised, and who has received a large amount of education material thru the mail, is an excellent prospect for a salesman. But, even when a salesman called on a possible purchaser who had not sent in an inquiry, the salesman could be reasonably sure that the prospect already knew of the encyclopedia, and that his interest to some extent must have been aroused in it. A very large number of sets of the encyclopedia were sold as a result of the excellent advertising supplementing the work of a considerable force of personal salesmen. Thousands of business houses use the magazines in part or in whole to produce "inquiries" which their salesmen "follow up" with personal calls.

7. *Use of farm journals*. In 1920 a little less than half of the population of the country (46 per cent) was rural. While many farmers read the general magazines, magazine circulation is chiefly in the cities and larger towns. Farm journals are probably the best media for reaching farm dwellers. The purposes for which farm journals are used does not differ greatly from those for which magazines are utilized. For a long time it was thought that farm publications should be used to advertise only things particularly adaptable to farm use. As a result, the advertising columns featured chiefly farm machinery, farm supplies, household utensils and mail-order advertisements for a variety of things that could be sold readily in the country but not so readily in the cities. Now, however, many advertisers are beginning to realize that farm wants do not differ greatly from city wants, and that anything in general use can be brought to the attention of farmers thru the medium of the farm journals more effectively than in any other way. Accordingly, the modern farm journal is likely to carry advertisements of breakfast food, clothing, investments, automobiles and all the other many things that are advertised in magazines. These advertisements are often exactly the same as the advertisements used in media circulating in the cities.

Farm journals, as has already been said, have for the most part territorial circulation. The extent to which farm journals as a class, and the extent to which any particular farm journal is to be used in a campaign depend on the thing advertised and the nature of the field to be reached. Some things cannot be used on the farm; it would be foolish to tell about them in farm papers. In other cases, the line of least resistance is to go to city dwellers who have ready access to stores handling the advertiser's good. In some states the farm population is negligible; in Rhode Island, for instance, only three and the: tenths of the population is classed as rural, and it; Massachusetts only live and two-tenths. To do mug business in North Dakota. on the other hand, farm trade is absolutely necessary, because eighty nine per cent of the people in that state are found on the farms and in very small towns.

8. *Use of trade, technical and class publications.* Trade, technical and class publications are used chiefly in advertising campaigns where it is advisable to reach and influence a certain class of people, Trade papers, therefore, contain advertisements chiefly of manufacturers and jobbers who Wish to in duce dealers to handle their goods. A technical publication for dentists carries advertisements chiefly of dental supply houses and of other advertisers who particularly wish the good-will of dentists. A class publication for teachers contains advertisements of books and appliances of particular interest to the teaching profession.

Trade, technical and class publications cannot sell space at as low a rate as newspapers and magazines having twenty or even a hundred times their circulation. Its actual cost, however, may be much less, say $50 a page in one issue of 15,000 circulation as against $7,000 for a page in a national weekly with 2,250,000 readers.

Trade papers are often used by manufacturers to tell dealers about advertising that is to be done to try to influence consumers. Other trade paper advertising is designed to induce orders from dealers. Trade paper advertising differs from consumer advertising in that in consumer advertising emphasis is put on the uses and quality of the article advertised, while in dealer advertising the emphasis is put on the profit to the dealer, the amount of consumer advertising that is being used to help the dealer move the goods and the general merchandising policies of the advertiser.

One of the interesting developments of trade paper advertising is the use of space in trade papers by the proprietors of other advertising media. Publishers of farm journals often feel that to assist their advertising patrons properly to distribute merchandise, the dealers must be acquainted with the advertising done in the farm papers; therefore the farm journals are taking liberal space in trade publications to advertise their own publications and their advertisers. One farm journal takes, a four-page insert once each month in the leading trade publications reaching the general stores, the grocery stores, the hardware dealers and the implement dealers of his territory. In these pages, the publisher of the farm journal tells the dealers. of the new campaigns about to be launched in his publication and reproduces some of the advertisements. This service is furnished without additional charge to all advertisers taking a certain amount of space in the farm publication. A great metropolitan newspaper takes regular space in trade papers each week, listing the products which ahead advertised in the newspaper and urging dealers to handle and push the advertised goods. As advertisers are coming to realize the power of the dealer to make or break any advertising campaign be and, as the trade papers increase in prestige and importance, they will be increasingly used as a delimit and valuable part of many advertising campaigns. e

9. *Use of foreign language publications.* Only 53.8 percent of the population of the United States are of native white parentage; 14. 5 percent are foreign born, and an additional 14 per cent are of foreign parentage. Many of the foreign born can be reached only by foreign language publications, and these same media can be used to reach effectively many others of foreign parentage and of mixed parentage. Primarily a foreign language publication is used by local retail advertisers who are of the same race as the readers of the publication. Other large Users of space are the department stores and other retail establishments that have a general appeal, and are as eager to get the trade of those born abroad as they are to get the trade of Native Americans. Obviously, a manufacturer making something that would appeal particularly to the people from a certain country would advertise in publications going primarily to those people. Few manufacturers are in this class, however. Nearly everything that is made has an appeal to people of all nationalities; accordingly, the foreign language newspapers are more and more being used by advertising manufacturers in the same way that they use publications in the English language.

10. *Use of directories*. Some advertisers trace their initial step back to directory advertisements. It is said that among directory advertisers the newspapers find their most profitable field for the development of newspaper advertisers.

Several attempts have been made from time to time to put directory advertising on a. basis allowing it to be used in national advertising campaigns. At present, directory advertising is for the most part local. Space in the five automobile Blue Books is often purchased by manufacturers engaged in a national campaign, and the time may come when telephone directory advertising will be used in the same way. The possibilities of telephone directories in a national campaign seem to be great. This medium gives a national advertiser an opportunity to publish the names, addresses 'and telephone numbers of his dealers in each community.

11. *Size of space in periodicals*. Probably the most difficult thing for any advertiser to determine in planning a campaign in periodicals is the size and space it is advisable for him to use. Some contend that small advertisements inserted often will bring more returns than large advertisements inserted less often. Others say that in the magazine the page is the ideal unit. Many advertisers now use the double spread exclusively and in special cases advertisers have used as many as ten pages in one issue of some of the most costly publications. As the number of advertisers increases, the size of space of each advertisement appears also to increase. In 1872 the average number of lines per advertisement in thy Century magazine was thirty-eight; in 1913, the average was 169. In 1890, about one-fifth of the total advertising space used in magazines consisted of full page advertisements. Today the ratio is better than one-half. In 1880, half-page spaces were used about two and one-half times as often as full-page spaces, in 1890, they were used less than twice as often, and now probably less than one-half as often. Professor Walter Dill Scott finds the mortality rate of advertisers is much greater among the users of small space than among the users of large space. He has made a tabulation of all the firms located west of Buffalo which advertised in the Ladies Home Journal during eight years, showing that the advertisers who used the largest size space lasted the longest. The following is the table:

Number of years the firms Average number of lines used continued to advertise annually by each firm

Number of years the firms continued to advertise		Average number of lines used annually by each firm	
1	year	56	lines
2	years	116	lines
3	years	168	lines
4	years	194	lines
5	years	192	lines
6	years	262	lines
7	years	218	lines
8	years	600	lines

Professor Scott comments as follows: "This would seem to indicate that, in general, if a firm uses 56 lines annually in the *Ladies' Home Journal*, the results will be so unsatisfactory that it will not try it again. If it uses 116 lines annually, it will be encouraged to attempt it the second year, but will then drop out. If, on the other hand, it uses 600 lines annually, the results will be so satisfactory that it will continue to use the same magazine indefinitely."

Many advertisers find their records of results increase in proportion to the size of space used. The Minnesota Harness Factory had, for several years, used quarter and eighth page advertisements in the leading farm papers of the northwest. The advertisements were all keyed and the cost per inquiry carefully watched. With the introduction of the tractor and the automobile the cost per inquiry in relation to a harness is rapidly on the increase. Realizing that size of advertisements makes a powerful impression on dealers and finding that their salesmen were not inclined to show proofs of the small advertisements, the Minnesota Harness Factory decided to use three quarter and full page advertisements only. The company expected to find quite a decided increase in the cost per inquiry, however. The cost per inquiry on the eighth and quarter page advertisements had averaged $2.52. The year that the three-quarter and full page advertisements were introduced, the cost per inquiry was cut to $1.67 on an average and the full page advertisements showed 75% more inquires than the three-quarter page advertisements. In addition to this, the salesmen took great pride in the new larger advertisements and the dealers responded proportion.

REVIEW
- When and how are newspapers ordinarily used by national advertisers? Magazines?
- If a manufacturer of smoking tobacco were considering media for a national advertising campaign, what are the chief arguments for and against his use of technical and class publications?
- What kinds of things can be advertised profitably in farm papers?
- Why does the publisher of a farm journal sometimes advertise in trade papers?

ADVISORY 12

THE USE of SIGNS

1. *Window trims*. Experienced advertisers in planning their campaigns seldom overlook anything that can help them to sell their goods. One of the "little things" of a campaign, but also one of the things that can do much to make the rest of the campaign effective, is the furnishing of various kinds of store signs to dealers. It is not enough to get the dealer to handle the goods and then to use periodicals to induce consumers to go to the dealer and ask for the things advertised. If this is all that is done, there is still a gap between the goods on the dealer's shelf and the impression made on the consumer by the periodical advertising. To bridge this gap the careful advertiser sees to it that there is something in the dealer's store to remind the visitor of things he has seen advertised in newspapers and magazines, and to stimulate his desire for them.

One of the important ways of aiding the dealer to move the advertiser's goods from his shelves is to furnish him with display material for his windows. The dealer's window is a valuable advertising medium. Live dealers realize the value of their windows; they will permit nothing, to go into them that does not possess distinct sales values; and usually they are willing to cooperate with the manufacturer who tries to aid them in selling the things they have in stock. Material that is to be used for display purposes in a dealer's window is called a window trim. Some national advertisers have made the window trim the principal feature of their advertising campaigns. Yale & Towne in introducing the Yale door check made effective use of a modification of the window trim. A Yale door check was placed on the front door of every retail store that had the article for sale. A cut-out paper arrow was pasted on the glass of the door, pointing to the door check, and bearing the words, "This is a complete door. It has a Yale door check affixed." Then black footsteps were stenciled on the sidewalk leading to the door. The door check, the door and the footsteps were reproduced in the national magazine advertising.

2. *The window trim and national sales week*. Some advertisers plan their campaigns to reach a climax in a certain specified week, and prepare elaborate window trims for dealers during that week. The "Hotpoint drive" illustrates this practice. During Hotpoint Week many thousands of dealers displayed in their windows Hotpoint electrical household appliances, and double-page advertisements appeared at the same time in the magazines. Sunkist Week of the California Fruit Growers' Association called for liberal use of window trims. Large advertisements in color were run in the leading magazines, full-page advertisements were placed in the newspapers, and dealers were furnished with window trim and other kinds of displays. The California Fruit Growers' Association paid for a half-page in each newspaper, with the understanding that the newspaper would obtain advertising of local dealers who handled Sunkist oranges and lemons, to fill the remaining half-page.

Most manufacturers of package goods find it advisable to prepare large dummies of their packages for window trimming purposes. These dummies are usually carried flat and are easily erected.

3. *The use of counter display.* Another popular form of dealer signs is the counter display. Some advertisers design their packages so that the boxes will make a natural counter display. Robert H. Ingersoll & Brother furnish an attractive counter rack from which Ingersoll watches may be suspended, thus, assuring the advertiser that his product is conspicuously brought to the attention of every store visitor.

Dealers prefer counter displays showing the goods themselves rather than signs that merely tell about the goods. One useful type of counter sign is sent out by a manufacturer of underwear. It is obviously impossible to display the underwear itself on a counter sign. The sign is about ten inches long by five inches high and triangular in shape. On the face in metal is the trade-mark name of the article, and on the reverse side, on a metal plate facing the clerk, are printed instructions regarding sizes and the best method of making a satisfactory fit.

In displaying certain articles, such as notions counter displays are of great importance. Articles of this type are likely to be put in a drawer or some other out-of-the-way place unless the manufacturer furnishes a sufficiently attractive display rack. The advertising of the Wisconsin Pearl Button Company centers largely around the cabinet furnished to dealers for the proper display of pearl buttons.

4. *How to get dealers to use signs*. There is much waste in the distribution of dealer signs. Some manufacturers ship a quantity of signs to every dealer who buys their goods. Many signs sent in this way are never used. Other manufacturers employ their own window trimmers to put up the signs, as it is found that in few cases will the dealer take time to place a window trim or even tack up a shelf card himself. As the life of a window trim is usually not longer than two weeks, some national advertisers, such as W. K. Kellogg and the National Biscuit Company, prefer making displays of dummy packages in the dealer's store above his shelves; these displays are usually left until the next housecleaning day, which may be six months or six years distant.

Several years ago the Printers Ink staff made an investigation of various kinds of dealer signs in an effort to obtain an estimate of their value, the attitude , of dealers and the requirements of a successful store display. The following are excerpts from this report:

Several dealers were prevailed on to give a frank statement of their attitude toward manufacturers' counter displays. Among them was Charles Holzhauer, of Newark, New Jersey, one of the leading pharmacists in the state of New Jersey and past president of the New Jersey Pharmaceutical Association. Mr. Holzhauer's idea of counter display hinges principally on the question of profit in the article to be displayed. He brings out the fact that many times a fine display has to be refused by him because he has a similar article under his own name which yields him a better profit. Commenting on the value of the counter display, he said: "Our counter space is valuable and we must put it to the best use. We use counter-display devices very often where the article does not conflict with other goods, and the profit is good. A great deal of money is wasted, I believe, in getting up material of this sort, which, falling into the dealer's hand, is at once consigned to the ash-barrel because he cannot sell the goods at a profit."

The report of the *Printers' Ink* investigators included records of plans and results of many different kinds of campaigns in which the attempt was made to induce dealers to use the various kinds of store displays furnished by manufacturers. One of the most interesting was the campaign of the Burson Knitting Company, manufacturers of hosiery. The cost of the entire campaign, including everything down to transportation charges, came to a trifle under three dollars a set. The way in which this company convinced 4,000 merchants that it was to their advantage to use the displays furnished by the manufacturer is told by one of the officers of the company:

First, we advertised the display in the trade papers which reached our field. We made it important enough to devote page spaces to it exclusively. We showed a photograph of the completed display and offered to tell a dealer how to get one. We did not offer to send the outfit, only to tell him how to get it. To all inquirers we sent a booklet, showing ten different ways in which the material could be combined to make ten different displays-and giving all the arguments for its use. A postcard was enclosed which entitled the dealer to an outfit without charge. The dealer was led first to inquire; then he got the book, which he was able to study at his leisure; and finally, when he thoroughly understood the proposition, he was led to ask for the material. If he wasn't convinced that it would pay him, he would never ask for it. I have been told by a merchant that I could have his windows for one of our big displays for so much a day. "Thank you," I usually replied, "but if your windows aren't worth any more than that we can't afford to give you the service. This display costs a great deal of money to build, and the company is paying my salary and that of my assistants simply to give this service to those merchants who are important enough to deserve it. It you don't think that your windows are worth a good many times twenty-five dollars a day to you, we'll have to accept your own valuation of them, but we are sorry to say that it isn't high enough to warrant us in placing the display in them."

5. *Most profitable fields for window and counter display.* The Printers' Ink investigation brought out the fact that as many as five different counter displays of well-known advertised brands were found at one time in one of the most exclusive shops in the Wall Street section of New York. Sealpackerchief handkerchiefs, Ingersoll watches, Ever-Ready razors and Paris garters were displayed in most of the leading men's furnishing shops. The report continues:

The hardware field is probably the most lucrative of them all. From interviews with the retailers, they all favor the counter displays and gladly accept them. This is due to the fact that many commodities in the hardware stores are bought on impulse. The dealer is aware of this situation, and realizes the necessity of the counter display. Many of the line-tool manufacturers realize that in order to have the purchaser appreciate quality they must display the tools in an artistic manner. The L.S. Starrett Company, Athol, Massachusetts, makes a fine display which it sends to the dealers. In order that the dealer may avail himself of this display, it is necessary for him to buy an assorted outfit amounting to $125. The company makes up several styles of cases; some are placed around the post in the store, others are hung on the wall. Other cases have drawers to hold surplus stock. Manufacturers are at liberty to draw their own conclusions from the data given. A few general conclusions may, however, be drawn. In order to secure representation, a counter display should fulfil the following conditions:

1. It should be distinctive, so that the dealer will feel that it will add something to his store.

2. It must be feature goods which the dealer really wants to sell; i.e., goods which afford him a good margin of profit.
3. It must be presented as a means to help him sell more goods; not as a bait to get him to buy more.

6. *Cooperating with dealers in buying signs*. With so many signs constantly offered to them, it is natural for some dealers to fail to realize the expense involved in the preparation of a sign and the actual money loss when a sign is not used or is thrown away. To obviate this difficulty some manufacturers, sell their signs to dealers. Of course the number of dealers who will pay for display material advertising a manufacturer's line is much smaller than the number of those who will use material sent them free on the other hand, when a dealer pays for displays the manufacturer can be certain that he will use them Many dealers realize the value of store displays of various sorts, but, because the cost of a single suit, able sign, window trim, or counter display would be almost prohibitive, they would not prepare a sign on their own initiative. The manufacturer is able to order in thousand lots, and can sell the sign to the dealer at a low price.

Sometimes a manufacturer finds out in advance from dealers how many of them will purchase signs, before having them made. He sends a photograph or description of the sign, and agrees to pay half of the cost of the display, perhaps, if the dealer will pay the other half. In such cases the dealer's name is usually printed on the sign as prominently as the manufacturer's if the sign is to be used outside the store. Fence signs, flange signs, posters and streetcar cards are often distributed in this way.

It is obvious that if a dealer is to pay his own money for signs, he must keenly appreciate their value and he must have unusual good-will for the things the signs are intended to advertise. The dealer who has an exclusive agency for an article is more likely to buy signs than a dealer who handles a line that is also found 1n all the other stores in town. One of the well known manufacturers of talking machines at one time prepared elaborate window trims at the factory, and sold them to dealers for five dollars each.

A common method of making dealers realize the value of display material is to give it to dealers only when they buy a certain quantity of goods. An initial order for a suitable amount of goods may entitle the dealer to a variety of kinds of advertising material, the selection to be made by the dealer and the salesman when the order is taken, or an order of so many cases at any time may entitle the dealer to certain specified kinds and amounts of signs.

Another method of impressing dealers with the value of advertising signs sent to them by manufacturers is to require them to pay for the space in local media, While the manufacturer furnishes the material. This applies to street-car cards and posters as well as newspaper advertising. Sometimes the manufacturer shares the cost of space.

7. *The use of posters*. The poster provides in the advertising campaign the element of large display. It goes out and arrests the attention of the possible consumer wherever he may be. Posters are usually intended to create a strong but a brief impression on the passer-by. The name of the product is strikingly displayed, with perhaps a picture linking up the name with the article or its use, and sometimes a terse selling point or two. The copy must be very brief, because people ordinarily do not stop to gaze at a poster; it must deliver its message while they are passing by. Posters are often used as supplementary mediums in a national campaign. Sometimes in districts where there is much illiteracy or where the periodicals have limited circulation, the striking poster display is almost the only medium an advertiser can profitably use. Posters have been found especially valuable in advertising motor accessories and automobiles. The appeal of the poster reaches the motorist at a time when he is likely to be thinking about his car and its needs.

Poster advertising space is sold on monthly con. tract. The advertiser usually furnishes the bill-posting company with the printed or lithographed sheets for posting, providing about twenty per cent more sheets than will be actually displayed in order to cover waste in posting and to permit new postings when old sheets are mutilated or destroyed.

A clever use of posting is employed by the Way Sagless Spring Company. This advertiser "travels" a poster display in Chicago. Monthly contracts are made for posters in different parts of the city. One month the posters appear on the North Side, the next month on the South Side, and the next month on the West Side. Each part of the city is billed regularly, but only for a month at a time.

8. *Use of painted bulletins*. Painted bulletins may be used in, practically, all the ways in which posters are used. They are ordinarily more expensive than posters

except when only a few displays are wanted. In this case the painted display is usually the cheaper because the advertiser is spared the expense of preparing lithographed sheets. In localities where poster or regular bulletin board displays are unavailable, advertisers find wall signs of advantage. Many advertisers make a custom of painting the blank walls of their local distributors. Just as it was formerly the custom among farmers to depend on national advertisers for the painting of their barns, so today many dealers rely on national advertisers for the painting of their store buildings. It is not an easy thing for a national advertiser to choose among posters, painted bulletins and wall signs. Most of the larger advertisers employ all three methods, choosing one or another for a community as local conditions may dictate.

9. *Use of street-car cards*. The street-car card is primarily an urban advertising medium. Although electric railways are fast stretching their lingers thru the rural districts, street-car advertising up to the present has been planned chiefly to reach the inhabitants of large cities and thickly populated districts. The street-car card is a sign, and is ordinarily used as any other sign-for bold display and small amount of copy, intended to make a quick, strong impression. Nevertheless it is possible to say more on a car card than on almost any other kind of sign medium.

Before 1900 space in street cars was usually sold by individual street railway companies to advertising companies which solicited advertisements locally. New car advertising all over the country is controlled for the most part by one company. The national advertiser can buy space in cars in all cities, if he wants to, on a single contract.

The present recognition of the possibilities of street. car advertising is largely attributable to the late Thomas Balmer. Before he was appointed advertising director of the Street Railways Advertising Association, street-car cards were usually thought of as permanent signs; very little copy was used and few changes of copy were employed. Mr. Balmer showed advertisers the possibilities of copy on street-car cards, possibilities of teaser campaigns and the advantages of inserting cards in series. Today some large national advertisers use as many as six different cards in the street cars of the same city during a month. A passenger transferring from car to car obtains a new impression or a reinforcement of an old impression in each car he enters.

As our cities become more congested and each individual becomes more dependent on the transit companies, advertisers have been quick to see the great possibilities of reaching people at central points in the transportation system. The elevated and subway posters, which are generally classed. With car cards, are fast becoming valuable advertising mediums. Many advertisers who use cards in the cars also use posters carrying the same designs, at the elevated and subway stations.

10. *Parades as advertising media.* The parade may be an advertising medium. When so used, it should be classed with the other sign media. Commercial parades seem to be increasing in popularity, despite the fact that most advertisers furnish floats under protest. A properly representative float for a parade in a large city can seldom be prepared for less than $200, and some of the most elaborately designed and lighted floats have cost as much as $20,000. When it is realized that a float is seldom used but once, the question of the advisability of this form of advertising is well worthy of consideration. An advertiser in answering this question should apply the same test that he would apply to any other medium: What is the cost per possible purchaser reached, and what is the prestige of the medium in the minds of possible purchasers? Is the crowd, which will see the float, made up of possible purchasers, and how large will that crowd be? Is the parade of sufficient importance in the minds of those watching it to make lack of representation by any advertiser noticeable? It has become a custom at the annual convention of the Associated Advertising Clubs of the World to have one large parade. This seems to set the stamp of highest authority, on the value of the parade as an advertising medium. The parade is purely a supplementary medium. It is of little value unless the advertiser is already known to his audience, because it is impossible in a parade to do more than give bold display to a name, a product or an idea.

Review
- In your opinion, should a manufacturer pay a dealer a use of window space to advertise the manufacturer's good?
- What particular kind of inside store sign would be best for a breakfast food? A brand of cigars? Shoes? Carpenters tools? What standard would you apply?
- What is your opinion of the value of advertising in moving picture theaters? Remember that different things influence different people. Be careful not to let possible personal prejudices influence your business judgment.
- What are the things that induce a dealer to use store signs supplied by manufacturers?

- How can the various kinds of sign advertising be closely connected with periodical advertising?

ADVISORY 13

CAMPAIGNS TO OBTAIN DISTRIBUTION

1. *Four kinds of campaigns.* Thus far in our study of advertising campaigns we have considered the elements of the campaign and the uses to which different advertising media are put. Now we are to consider the various things the campaign-may accomplish and the ways in which the advertiser adapts publicity methods to make them conform to his particular purposes.

In general, there are four distinct kinds of advertising campaigns, apart from the campaigns of retail stores:

1. Campaigns to obtain distribution
2. Campaigns to obtain dealer cooperation
3. Mail-order campaigns
4. Campaigns to influence public sentiment.

In the present chapter and in the three that follow it, we are to study separately each of the four principal classes of advertising campaigns. We are concerned, first, with campaigns to obtain distribution.

2. *Should advertising precede distribution?* For years advertisers have sought a universally applicable answer to the question, "Shall I advertise in order to obtain distribution, or shall I try to get distribution before I advertise?" The manufacturer who advertises to consumers before he has general distribution of his product, believes that he cannot induce dealers to stock his goods until the

dealers have seen his efforts to create consumer demand or until consumers have proved that there is a demand by actually going into stores and asking for the advertised goods.

It is clear, however, that advertising preceding distribution is bound to result in much waste. If a consumer has his interest and desire for a new product amused, asks his dealer for it, and is told that the latter does not carry it, he may not be Willing to wait until the dealer can order it for him. The newly aroused interest is likely to be killed. Furthermore, most advertisers find that advertising in periodicals alone is often not enough to arouse interest in something new; it must be supplemented by store signs and the active work of the dealer. For these reasons many manufacturers try to, get general distribution for their goods before doing a great deal to bring people into stores to ask for them.

The problem of whether advertising or distribution should come first seems to be similar to the problem of the Irishman's boots; they were so tight he could not get them on until he had worn them a year. The problem is not unsolvable, however. If it were, there would be no successful advertising campaigns. Advertisers now recognize that neither distribution nor advertising must necessarily come first; in many cases it is possible to get distribution and to arouse consumer interest simultaneously. Mr. William H. Ingersoll says, in Printers' Ink:

Neither distribution nor demand can precede the other without loss. If we are going to wait for distribution, we shall wait forever, or nearly forever. On the other hand, if we are going to create a demand without distribution, without advertising-then again we are going to delay the time that we reach the success to which we are entitled. In other words', the most economical, most efficient way, in my opinion, of handling this subject of distribution and demand is to go ahead in a moderate way and advertise, take the sales methods that are at hand, and keep the demand going by getting all the distribution you can.

Dealers are influenced both by advertising that is being used and by advertising which the manufacturer convinces them he is about to use. Salesmen often carry portfolios of present or projected advertising, which they show to dealers as evidence of the part the manufacturer is willing to play in helping dealers to move goods from their shelves. These portfolios sometimes show not only the advertisements themselves, the list of media and the dates when the advertisements are to appear, but also the circulation of every medium in each dealer's own towns.

3. *Starting on a small scale.* It is not necessary for a manufacturer to begin his consumer campaign with national advertising. An article of universal consumption is seldom introduced in all parts of the country at the same time. Ordinarily a relatively small territory is selected as a "tryout market." Intensive sales effort is used there to interest dealers, and this is backed by various kinds of local advertising. It is entirely possible to send a force of sales. men to a certain city to work with the dealers, and to start a newspaper, street-car and poster campaign in the same city simultaneously with the arrival of the salesmen.

Consider the problem of a manufacturer of flour. Unless he had tremendous resources he would not consider attempting a national campaign until he had built up distribution and consumer demand by starting out in a single center, and then branching out gradually into adjacent territories. If he were strong enough to begin with a section of the country instead of with a small section of a state, he might plan his campaign so as to make the successive steps in its development coincide with the divisions of the country recognized by the Federal Reserve bank system. There are twelve Federal Reserve banks, each centering a district which is largely tributary to it. If large sections of the country are to be used as units in the campaign, probably no better divisions than those established by the Federal banking system could be found. The accompanying map shows the twelve divisions of the country, the amount paid for flour by consumers, when flour is $10 a barrel, and the percent of total consumption which is represented by the expenditures for flour in each district.

4. *A flour campaign.* A manufacturer usually commences with his home territory as a tryout market. Assume that a flour manufacturer has a factory in Kansas City, the center of Federal Bank District No. 10. He will send salesmen to dealers, and he will choose advertising mediums reaching flour consumers in Kansas, Nebraska, Wyoming, Colorado, and parts of New Mexico, Oklahoma and Missouri. After he has worked up his business in this district, he will probably expand into Federal District No. 8, establishing a district agency in St. Louis in an effort to obtain his share of the $118,305,500 market in this district.

Other conditions being favorable, he may next consider the Chicago district, the Dallas district or the Minneapolis district. In each case he will use localized media, such as newspapers, billboards, street cars and farm papers supplemented by sampling and possibly direct-by-mail advertising, repeating the same campaign, changed to fit local conditions, in each territory.

After the manufacturer has covered, say, four or five of the trade territories, and has obtained What he considers satisfactory distribution in each, he will be in a position to consider national advertising, using national magazines, national farm journals, a schedule of national posters, or a schedule of the leading newspapers in the large cities, the circulation of which linked together will blanket the country.

In this case, as in many others, national advertising follows a long period of local advertising coupled with careful cultivation of dealers. For many products any other plan than this would be too wasteful and too expensive.

5. *Distribution for an article of limited consumption*. In marketing an office appliance sold thru Stationers, a manufacturer would proceed in a very different way from that in which a flour campaign would have to be conducted. National advertising could begin almost at once, because he could bring a direct appeal to all the possible distributors within a short time. Instead of a total of 25,000,000 families and 350,000 dealers, as in the case of the flour manufacturer, the total consumer market would be only about 1,000,000. If he wished to distribute thru the stationers he would need to reach 38,500, while if he wished to limit his distribution to one agent in each city with a population over 5,000 a complete distribution would be less than 1,500. In order to reach the number of dealers in automobile supplies he might send salesmen to dealers in the larger cities; and appeal to the others by direct advertising of various sorts-strong sales letters, a catalog and reproductions of the consumer advertising. Probably he would also use the advertising columns of the trade papers in order to talk directly with dealers.

6. *Dangers of overstocking*. Some manufacturers in their eagerness to make large sales to dealers, induce them to buy more goods than they can sell within a reasonable time. At the beginning of a campaign the dealer is seldom in a position to determine for himself just how many of the new products he will be likely to sell. The manufacturer should see: that he does not stock too heavily. An overstock often means the loss of the dealer's good-will, and it usually results in disastrous price-cutting. The men who are overstocked and who cut prices will scarcely be willing to order again when their stock is gone, and the dealers who do not cut prices will see their trade leaving them and will focus their resentment on m, goods. In either case, the manufacturer loses. A manufacturer does not conduct an elaborate campaign to induce first sales only; his profits must come from reorders,

and reorders are received only when the dealer has been treated fairly-when prices and profits are right, when the manufacturer has done his part to interest consumers, and when the dealer's first stock has been large enough to satisfy immediate demands but small enough to permit a rapid turnover of the money invested in it.

The Procter & Gamble Company, when it introduced Crisco, sent free to every grocer in the country six cans of the product. Gratuitous distribution of small sample stocks is certainly an almost ideal way of inducing dealers to handle a new line of goods, but it is too expensive for many manufacturers to use.

7. *When distribution preceded advertising*. When, in 1906, William Wrigley, jumped into advertising with an appropriation of $250,000, many people called it plunging. They did not know about the long years of preparatory work in an effort to obtain a nation-wide distribution. Practically all the $250,000 was spent in out-door display, street-car cards and window trims. Before a cent of this appropriation was spent almost complete distribution had been obtained thru direct advertising to dealers. Mr. Wrigley started in business with a capital of $32. He attempted distribution thru premiums. His first venture was in lamp chimneys. He filled lamp chimneys full of gum and sold the gum, throwing in the lamp chimney. He studied dealers, and offered as premiums the things they really wanted. A certain retail grocer needed, say, a special counter scale. Along came a circular from Wrigley offering an attractive scale free if the grocer would go to his wholesaler and buy $15 worth of gum.

Thus, step by step, Wrigley obtained a foothold. Then he established a great direct-by-mail advertising campaign to dealers. Multigraphed circulars were mailed every thirty days to 250,000 dealers whom Mr. Wrigley wished to get into line. If 12,000 of these prospects were turned into customers in any given month and the prospect list thus reduced to 238,000, an addition was immediately made to the list so that the number of names was brought up to 250,000. The list of dealer prospects was always maintained at the 250,000 mark.

The national advertising did not commence until the company had been in business fourteen years. Therefore, when the quarter of a million advertising campaign was undertaken, the foundation of distribution had been laid. This foundation was laid so successfully and the business showed such a fast, steady increase after the national advertising had appeared that before the end of 1916 the company was spending two million dollars a year in advertising.

8. *Using established good-will to obtain distribution*. When Mr. Wrigley put Doublemint gum on the market, he was able to use the thousands of dealers who were already handling his earlier brand. In less than sixty days 500,000 distributers for the new gum were obtained. These were enlisted from the 800,000 who were then selling Spearmint. Each of these 800,000 received a coupon entitling him to one box of the new gum, provided the dealer handed it to his jobber with an order for one box of Spearmint before the time-limit indicated on the coupon expired.

The William Wrigley, J r., Company redeemed these coupons from the jobbers at the regular price of sixty cents a box, thus allowing the jobber his usual twelve cents profit; or, to put it in another way, the company paid the jobber twelve cents to deliver the sample box to the dealer. The expense was very great; in all, $300,000 was paid out in redemption money to secure distribution, but for every box of the new gum given away, a box of the old brand was sold; in this way the expense was largely offset. The plan enabled the company to take advantage of distribution already secured, and this immediate distribution made possible immediate consumer advertising on a national scale. Furthermore, by getting immediate distribution the danger of substitution was greatly reduced. If the company had started to advertise with haphazard distribution, dealers might have been inclined to talk their customers into using other gums, and the new brand would have been deprived of an opportunity to demonstrate its merit.

REVIEW

- Should distribution or consumer advertising come first?
- Is it wise to try to introduce a new product in all parts of the country at once? Why? What is the alternative?
- Is it advisable to launch a new article by selling it both to dealers and consumers at a special introductory low price? What would be your probable action if you paid twenty cents for a new shaving soap, only to find when you re-ordered that the price was twenty-five cents?
- Some people contend that a dealer should be stocked just as heavily as possible with a new line of goods, on the theory that the more he has, the harder he will try to sell them. What do you think of this policy? Would your

answer be different if the question referred to an old, long established line of goods which the dealer had handled for years?

ADVISORY 14

CAMPAIGNS TO OBTAIN DEALER COOPERATION

1. *Place of dealer in the campaign.* The attitude of the dealer is one of the vital considerations in planning an advertising campaign. The success of the campaign depends to a great extent on the degree to which dealers will be willing to cooperate with the manufacturer in the sale of his goods. Sometimes the dealer will not cooperate. If he is openly antagonistic, the campaign can scarcely be successful; if he is indifferent, success can be bought only at a great price. Some manufacturers seem to think the dealer owes them cooperation-that he should lend his active efforts to encourage any sort of campaign for the promoting of sales thru retail stores. This attitude on the part of manufacturers is responsible for much dealer antagonism. The dealer resents attempts at coercion; he resents the implication that he must give his active support to any manufacturer simply because the manufacturer elects to distribute thru the dealer and conducts some sort of campaign to help the dealer sell his goods. Dealers cannot handle every line that is offered them; they must make careful selection from the almost countless things that manufacturers seek to induce them to push; and they are likely to put their Alerts behind the products of those manufacturers who wisely seek cooperation by proving themselves most willing to cooperate unselfishly with dealers. The attitude of the advertiser and the dealer toward each other is more wholesome than it used to be, but there is still room for improvement in the understanding of the dealer by the advertiser and in the understanding of the advertiser by the dealer.

2. *Three periods of dealer cooperation.* At the beginning of the twentieth century many manufacturers seemed to think the attitude of the dealer did not count-that the force of advertising with resulting demand on the part of consumer

would require dealers to handle advertised goods, and that competition among dealers for the trade in such lines would make it necessary for each dealer to push them. This was the period of "Force the dealer." There was much talk about using advertising as a club to compel the sale of advertised goods, whether dealers wanted to sell them or not. Some advertisers were successful in "forcing the dealer," Although at very great cost. Others found that it is unwise to try to make dealers do something they do not want to do. It was discovered that many dealers can induce their customers to buy What they recommend, regardless of an original intention on the part of consumers to buy something else. "Forcing the dealer" in general proved to be an expensive and wasteful method of inducing sales, even in the few cases in which it was successful.

3. *Period of "Bluff the dealer."* Following the "Force the dealer" period, which lasted for about ten years, came another, similar to it, but marking a sort of half-way stage between the crude methods of the early days and the more intelligent methods of obtaining cooperation in vogue today. This might be called the period of "Bluff the dealer." The advertiser began to have some conception of the dealer's attitude; he did not ignore the dealer's opinions—he did not merely advertise to consumers and trust to consumer demand to force the dealer into line. He began to cater to the dealer and to try to make him eager to have a part in the large sales which were expected as a result of the manufacturer's advertising He did this by talking grandly to the dealer about the large scale of the projected advertising campaign. He took space for his consumer advertisements in mediums that the dealers were sure to read. He did everything, in short, to impress the dealer with the importance of the manufacturer and with the size and probable effectiveness of his advertising. The advertiser was not really bluffing; he really carried out his largely advertised advertising plans, but he deluded himself, and he tried to delude the dealer, into thinking that those plans, with nothing added, were enough by themselves to deserve and to obtain the cooperation of the trade.

4. *Period of "Help the dealer."* The third and the present period of dealer cooperation is the period of "Help the dealer" Its basis is the idea that dealers must be helped and educated, rather than forced or bullied. The period came into existence when advertisers generally began to realize that the dealer is not a mere distributing machine, but that he is a powerful force to be reckoned with. In the early days of national advertising, "consumer demand" was assumed to be a thing of prime importance. If enough consumers could be influenced to want advertised goods, the problem of the dealers would take care of itself. We hear less of

consumer demand nowadays. The modern phrase is "consumer acceptance." National advertising is no longer expected to do all the work of making sales. It has been proved in many instances that advertising does not create such an intense desire for advertised articles that consumers insist on having those articles or nothing. Dealers can and do switch demand; they can and do exert a tremendous influence on what consumers buy. The function of national advertising is no longer simply to cause consumers to "demand" advertised goods; its chief function often is to impress advertised goods on the minds of consumers so forcefully that when those goods are suggested to them by dealers, the dealer suggestions, added to the impression created by the advertising, will induce them quickly and with little sales effort to "accept" the advertised article.

Of course, Consumer acceptance is not the sole purpose of all consumer campaigns for products sold thru dealers. Yet it is sufficiently universal and sufficiently important a purpose to color almost all the modern attempts to obtain dealer cooperation, dealer is to do his part in inducing consumer acceptance, he must have a degree of good-will toward the manufacturer and his goods which is very different from his former frequent attitude of resentment or indifference

5. *The spirit of sales cooperation.* There are many methods of inducing dealers to push advertised goods at the bottom of all the successful ones, however, there is one common characteristic. The manufacturer who really gets active good-will is the one who convinces dealers that he is willing to help them if they will help him. He shows that the things he asks the dealer to do are calculated to help the dealer at least as much as they help the manufacturer; and, in the most successful campaigns, service to dealers greatly over. shadows the manufacturer's desire to increase immediately the sale of his goods. Of course, whenever a manufacturer really helps a dealer, he creates good. will that is bound to result in his favor, and, if the help takes the form of education in better business methods, those methods will help the manufacturer just as much as they will help the dealer.

6. *Influence of quality of goods.* The manufacturer who wants dealer cooperation must first see to it that the quality of his goods is such that the retailer will recognize it and the retailer's customers will be satisfied with their purchases. The retailer wants permanent trade; he can get it only when his customers are pleased with their purchases and come back for more. Therefore, the first thing the dealer looks for is quality.

7. *Profit as an inducement to cooperate*. After quality, the dealer wants profit. The price he pays for goods and the price at which he can sell them must be far enough apart to cover all his expenses of doing business and to leave him a satisfactory profit besides. Many advertising campaigns have failed because the item of profit was overlooked or because the margin allowed was too small. No matter how much a manufacturer tries to help dealers to sell his goods, no matter how effective his advertising, no matter how much quality he puts into the line, if the profit is not right the dealer will not cooperate.

8. *Importance of quick stock turnovers*. After quality and profit, the dealer wants to be assured regarding the ease with which the goods will sell. Modern merchandising requires small stocks and quick turnovers. Besides putting quality into his goods and selling them at the right price, the manufacturer can help the dealer to achieve quick turnovers in two ways: First, he can adopt some selling plan that will make complete stocks of his goods easily accessible to dealers, so they can order frequently and in small quantities. Second, he can help the dealer to move the goods off his shelves. In achieving this second purpose advertising plays a large part. Various methods of inducing dealer cooperation by means of advertising are described in the following pages.

9. *Educating the dealer and his sales people*. One of the best ways of arousing the interest of dealers is to teach them the points of interest about the things they sell. A carpet manufacturer sent to all his dealers and thei1 sales people a booklet entitled "What I Learned About Carpets." It told in a lively way the experiences of a retail salesman that visited a carpet factory for the first time. Certainly the retailer who read this story could sell carpets more intelligently than he could before, and he would feel a real interest in the manufacturer who had helped him learn more about his goods. Many manufacturers go to great lengths to interest dealers in their lines by teaching them the selling points. Moving pictures of manufacturing processes are displayed before groups of store employees; booklets are distributed; traveling exhibits are routed from store to store; salesmen give lectures to buyers and sales people; and many similar methods are used to obtain cooperation by arousing interest.

A new kind of education for retailers has for its purpose, not primarily increased sales of any given manufacturer's goods, but, rather, increased sales and increased profits for the dealer in his business as a whole. The Printz-Biederman Company, manufacturers of women's garments, formerly provided a correspondence course in retail selling for the employees of the suit and cloak departments of its dealers. The course was a broad one; it taught the best methods of selling women's garments in general, and referred only incidentally to the product of the company that prepared the course. A manufacturer of sad-irons for a time distributed a correspondence course in advertising for the retail dealer, covering everything from study of the market to copy-writing, methods of display and the selection of media. The manufacturer of Ingersoll watches prepared, and distributed free to his dealers, a complete system of cost accounting for jewelry stores. Broad-minded, unselfish educational efforts of this sort represent a long step in advertising from the days when "Force the dealer" was the slogan. They promise much for the future of dealer-manufacturer relations.

10. *Campaigns to increase the sales of related products*. Strategy in advertising is expressed in a variety of ways. The advertiser who offers a free course in accounting for his dealers is a strategist of the first order. His final, and legitimately selfish, purpose is entirely overshadowed by an unselfish desire to be of real service to his distributers. In the same class is the manufacturer of one product who advertises another for the benefit of his dealers. They both carry a principle of broad-minded American life, that of mutual helpfulness, into business relations. They both prove the growing realization in business of the old truth that the one who profits most is the one who serves most. The Bemis Bag Company manufactures containers for flour. Yet it does not advertise bags. Just before the Food Administration introduced "Wheatless days" it was advertising to increase the consumption of flour, because its business can increase only the business of the millers of the country increase; The Bemis Company published advertisements in the leading magazines and newspapers showing the nutriment in white flour, and urged housewives to make more liberal use of it. The object of the campaign was twofold. First, the obvious object is to increase the consumption of white flour, if that is possible. But the other object, and the one which was undoubtedly a great deal more definitely realized, was to get the good-will of millers. The miller feels that the manufacturer is attempting to render him a real service. The manufacturer does not come to the miller saying, "I want your bag business." He says, "I'm going to do everything I can to increase your flour business. Then you will have to use more bags. If you buy them from me, I shall appreciate it. I expect to succeed only by assisting you to success."

Thru advertising, the business men of the country in all lines, whether they are retailers, jobbers or manufacturers, are coming to understand one another better, and to know the real meaning of cooperation and service.

11. *Three kinds of "dealer helps."* The forms of advertising most generally used by a manufacturer in his effort to gain dealer cooperation are those that help the dealer to tell the public about the manufacturer's goods. These helps, aside from the educational work already described, are of three kinds store signs, assistance of various sorts in the retailer's newspaper advertising and assistance in his direct advertising.

12. *Dealers' newspaper advertising.* One of the first attempts of manufacturers to obtain dealer cooperation was by offering assistance to retailers in the preparation of their newspaper advertising. The average retailer has had little opportunity to study advertising carefully; or he is usually busy with a multitude of store details, and he thinks he has not the time to devote to the writing of advertisements, even if he had the training to do so. As a result of these two conditions much retail advertising up to a few years ago, particularly in the smaller communities, was weak and ineffective. Taking advantage of this situation, national advertisers offered to help the retailer produce advertisements that would really attract trade.

The first kind of advertising help offered to the dealer was a complete advertisement of manufacturer's goods, electrotyped and ready for insertion in the dealer's papers, with only a small place left blank for the dealer's name and address. Complete advertisements of this sort have been, and still are, widely used. Many manufacturers prepare them and many dealers use them. This advertising is often better than the dealer could prepare. for himself, and sometimes the dealer would use no newspaper advertising at all if it were not for the plated advertisements he receives from manufacturers. To that extent, the material is valuable.

It has the great disadvantage, however, of representing the manufacturer and his goods rather thank the dealer and his store. An advertisement prepared for a thousand stores can certainly not reflect the individuality of any one of them. A realization of this fact is inducing many dealers to refuse to use plated advertisements from manufacturers, and it is inducing many manufacturers to find some other methods of bringing about dealer cooperation. The sincere, frank recommendation of the dealer, no matter how crudely expressed, is often worth much more to the readers of a paper than even the strongest appeal of an advertisement obviously written by a manufacturer.

13. *Advertisements that represent the dealers*. When the manufacturer wishes to present complete advertisements to his distributers, a better plan than the sending of electrotyped advertisements is to send sheets of paper to the dealer, showing suggested advertisements of the manufacturer's goods. The dealer can use the suggested wording if he wants to, or he can change it to suit himself. When cuts are used the dealer can get them on request or for a nominal charge. Dealers like this kind of advertising assistance. The only objection to it from the manufacturer's point of view is that most dealers, when they use the suggested advertisements at all, use them without alteration. To this extent, this advertising is open to the same objections as the older type of plated advertisements.

Complete advertisements furnished to dealers, either plated or simply printed as suggestions, may deal entirely with the goods of the manufacturers supplying them, or they may contain sales talk about other things in the dealer's stock. In the former case, many dealers resent the obvious selfishness of the manufacturer's appeal. They are much more likely to give their support to a manufacturer who helps them sell other things in addition to his own product.

Some manufacturers supply dealers with complete advertisements, but make no attempt to prepare stock advertisements. When a retailer asks help, his store and his particular problems are studied by correspondence and thru the reports of salesmen. As a result the manufacturer's advertisement department is able to write advertisements that just as truly represent the dealer as if he wrote them himself. This kind of assistance is about the maximum of advertising service that a manufacturer can give a retailer in his attempt to obtain cooperation. For many manufacturers, however, it is prohibitively expensive.

14. *Furnishing parts of advertisements*. The majority of advertisers have abandoned the attempt to supply dealers with complete newspaper advertisements. A common practice now is to furnish cuts for illustrations only. The dealer receives sheets showing stock cuts illustrating the manufacturer's goods. He selects what he wants and uses them in any way he wants to in his advertisements. A commendable modification of this practice is to send with the book of cuts suggested sentences or paragraph that can be used by the dealer when he

publishes the cuts. If these paragraphs are written in a lively way, and if the dealer is assured that they are merely Intended to help him and not to bind him to any particular phraseology, he is likely to use them.

Several stove manufacturers have made a practice of furnishing cuts illustrating almost everything in a retail hardware store, and even of writing copy to go with the cuts. They asked nothing for the services, merely putting their own trade-marks, often in inconspicuous places, on the cuts or copy furnished.

Some manufacturers furnish street-car cards and sheets for bill-posting to dealers who use these media. Others simply make suggestions for any kind of advertising a dealer may wish to undertake.

15. *Assistance in dealers direct advertising.* Many retailers find that direct advertising to their customers or possible customers, either alone or in combination with newspaper and sign advertising, is a valuable method of building business. They often find it just as difficult to prepare their own direct advertising, however, as to prepare their newspaper advertisements. Accordingly, some manufacturers help them in this form of publicity. The great clothing companies send out style books to lists of names furnished them by their dealers. Each book carries the dealer's imprint, and usually is accompanied by a letter, prepared by the manufacturer, but signed by the dealer. Modifications of this plan are used by manufacturers in other lines. Doubtless the plan is effective, but great care must be used if the manufacturer wishes consumers really to believe that the direct advertising carries the sincere indorsement of his local dealer. A dealer's direct advertising that is obviously furnished by a manufacturer is not so effective as that which carries some ear-marks of the dealer's personality.

16. *Manufacturers' consumer advertising.* We have described a number of ways in which advertising may be used by a manufacturer to induce dealers to cooperate with him in the sale of his goods. All of them are good when employed wisely, and all of them are widely used. But none of the special forms of inducements to dealers should blind the manufacturer to the greatest inducement of all-persistent, effective advertising by the manufacturer, directed toward the consumer, slowly but steadily making the manufacturer, his goods, his trade-mark and his selling points known to the public and, if not actually creating insistent consumer demand, at least paving the way for ready acceptance of the manufacturer's product when any effort at all is put behind it by the dealer. This form of advertising assistance,

more than any other, helps the dealer to make sales quickly and at little expense, and, when it is used for a product that has quality and that gives the dealer a satisfactory profit, it is usually successful in inducing valuable cooperation.

Several years ago the Northern Pine Manufacturers Association tried to overcome the shrinking demand for pine by advertising to the trade only. The results of the campaign were not satisfactory, and the world of housebuilders was left to persist in its belief that all the white pine was used up, or, if some was left, that it was too expensive for ordinary use. The Southern Cypress Manufacturers' Association realizing that "the consumer is king," began to advertise to win the patronage of consumers. National magazines and farm journals were used extensively. In all, an aggregate of 5,500,000 circulation was employed in consumer publicity. The result has been a large increase in the use of cypress. The association purchased space in the trade publications, not so much for the purpose of urging the trade to use more cypress, as to explain to the trade the consumer advertising it was conducting.

This successful experience of the Southern Cypress Manufacturers' Association led to the organization among the Northern Pine Manufacturers' Association of a white pine bureau, which began to advertise the advantages of white pine to consumers. The effort was successful from the start. Dealers, realizing that the manufacturers were advertising to increase their sales, put forth additional effort, began to use the dealer helps furnished them, and even inaugurated campaigns of their own in local territories to counteract the impression that the supply of white pine is exhausted, and to show the advantages of white pine over other woods.

Dealers Cooperation can be obtained by hard work, fair treatment and a real willingness to serve. But the dealer does not ordinarily give full cooperation unless the manufacturer does his part by advertising to the consumer.

17. *Dealers meet advertisers half-way.* The degree of cooperation that may be expected from intelligent effort on the part of manufacturers is indicated by the success of "national advertising weeks," fostered by some of the magazines in cooperation with manufacturers. The plan is for the dealers in a town during a "national advertising week" to feature nationally advertised goods in their stores, their windows and their newspaper advertising. During such a week one dealer turned a whole floor of his store into a special exhibit of 115 booths showing

nationally advertised goods. Each booth was in charge of a demonstrator. The manufacturers bore the expense of decorating and equipping the booths. In return, the dealer spent $10,000 of his own money in newspaper advertising and in furnishing heat, light and special sales people. Every visitor to a booth signed a register. The names were later furnished to the manufacturers, who agreed to send direct advertising to these persons. The results were satisfactory both to the manufacturers and to the dealer.

All retailers cannot cooperate in this extensive way, but most of them, to the extent that their resources permit, are willing to cooperate with manufacturers who give them quality and profit, and who offer intelligent help in solving the great problem of attracting and holding trade.

REVIEW

- What is the difference between "consumer demand" and '"consumer acceptance"? What are the things, apart from advertising: that tend to induce dealer cooperation?
- If you were a retailer, what tests would you apply in determining the relative acceptability of the many things manufacturers would offer to do for you to obtain your cooperation?
- If the business with which you are connected sells a product or service thru distributors, how is their cooperation obtained?
- How might it be obtained?
- How does dealer distribution differ from dealer cooperation?
- Can the same methods be used in obtaining both?

ADVISORY 15

MAIL-ORDER CAMPAIGNS

1. *Kinds of mail-order campaigns*. There are three general kinds of mail-order campaigns: (1) The campaign of a mail-order specialty house, which sells one line of goods or service, or several closely allied lines, and which uses the mails to make sales as part of the established house policy. In this class are mail-order distributors of jewelry, furs, clothing, food products and thousands of other things sold to consumers by mail. (2) Similar to the campaign of the mail-order specialty house is that of a manufacturer who introduces his goods to consumers by mail, but Who later expects to distribute them thru dealers. (3) The third kind of mail-order campaign is conducted by the establishment that tries to sell a great variety of things by mail. In this class are such mail-order distributors as Sears, Roebuck & Company, Montgomery Ward & Company, and the city department stores, not so many as formerly, that sell by mail as well as over the counter.

As far as purpose and method are concerned, the first two classes may be grouped together. The purpose of both is to make sales as the direct result of the advertisements. Frequently the reader is urged to send his money or to order at once, usually with the promise that the money will be refunded if the purchase proves unsatisfactory. At other times, periodical advertising is intended only to arouse interest, and the reader is urged to ask for further information; the sale is then made with the aid of follow up letters and booklets. Sometimes both appeals are combined in one advertisement: "Send only $2. or ask for booklet."

The appeal of the third kind of mail-order campaign is different from that of the other two. The house that sells many different kinds of things by mail usually advertises in periodicals chiefly for the purpose of getting a list of names of people to whom a catalog may be sent. The catalog of such houses is relied on to make the sales. A few direct orders may come as a result of periodical advertisements that feature particular things, but, in general, the periodical advertising is intended to distribute catalogs rather than to make immediate sales.

We have divided mail-order campaigns into three groups on the basis of the differences of appeal and method. Still another classification might be made. Some mail-order campaigns are directed to consumers; others are directed to dealers. Butler Brothers and the Baltimore Bargain House are examples of wholesale houses selling by mail to dealers. We are to consider chiefly mail-order campaigns of those who sell to consumers; the methods of such campaigns differ but slightly from the methods of selling by mail to dealers.

2. *The mail-order specialty advertiser.* One has only to open any magazine of general circulation to find offers by mail-order specialty houses representing nearly every class of human wants, including cigars, lessons in nursing, apples, furnaces, books and even automobiles.

Canned fish does not sound like a highly promising mail-order proposition, but the Frank E. Davis Come Pany of Gloucester, Massachusetts, has made a success in this rather unpromising field by advertising its products at first in the general magazines and more recently also in a considerable number of newspapers. The president is thus quoted in a newspaper advertisement:

Buying fish by mail is simply the working out of the old principle that "a straight line is the shortest distance between two points." And in this case the "straight-line" way-the direct way-is the easy, safe and satisfactory way. Ever since that day back in the early eighties, when I sent out my first pail of mackerel, I've kept this one thought firmly in mind: "My fish must always be better than folks can buy in their local stores or I can't hope to sell it." The fish which your dealer offers is simply what he can buy from the middleman. He is too far from the source of supply to obtain selected grades of fish. I am right on the ground-I get the first choice of the best catches-clean and pack everything, fresh from the ocean in the most sanitary and best equipped buildings possible to construct. Then it is shipped direct to you. No matter where you live, you can have from me, for your home table, just as good fish as we folks here on the sea can enjoy it is generally agreed that there are many articles that cannot be sold profitably by mail, and moreover the cost of making mail sales seems to be steadily rising.

3. *Requirements of mail-order specialty house*. As has been said already, not everything can be sold profitably by mail. In considering the advisability of launching a mail-order specialty business one of the first questions to be asked is, "Are my possible customers near enough to me so that the transportation charges on the smallest unit will not materially affect my price in competition?"

When the parcel post was established, many new opportunities were opened for mail-order specialty houses. The specialty shoe house is an example. By shipping by parcel post, one mail-order shoe house found its average cost of transportation was eleven cents a pair, against, a previous charge of thirty cents, the difference allowed a good profit and induced many concerns to go into the business. While some advertised in the farm journals, most of them bought special lists of names and then advertised directly with catalogs and letters.

The matter of transportation cost, however, is only one of the many expenses to be considered in selling by mail. Most things can be sold by mail if enough money is spent in the process. The great problem of the prospective mail-order advertiser is: "Is there sufficient margin between the cost to manufacture and the price at which I can sell my goods by mail to Pay all the expenses of this kind of selling and still have me a profit?" Many mail-order campaigns have failed because this question has not been properly considered in advance. A manufacturer once at« tempted to sell-a talking machine attachment by mail for one dollar. His manufacturing cost was less than fifty cents, and he assumed that the difference between cost and selling price was ample to cover all expenses, and leave him a good profit besides. He found that it actually cost seventy cents to make each sale; he was losing twenty cents on every article sold.

4. *Influence of style camera*. One of the reasons why people buy wearing apparel by mail is that they feel they get better styles when they buy, sometimes from distant firms, thru the mails than when they buy in their own communities. Because New York is supposed to originate, or to be the first to import styles in women's clothing, such mail-order houses as the National Cloak and Suit Company and Bellas, Hess Company do a large business with women all over the United States. The desire to buy in the style centers is responsible for much mail-order buying.

Within ten years one New York mail-order house has built up an exclusive ladies' ready-to-wear mail order business with 2,500,000 customers, and is spending over $2,000,000 a year on catalogs and other advertising. This company issues live catalogs-a large one for spring and summer, another large one for fall and winter, and three smaller catalogs for special lines. The large books go out in editions of 2, 500 000 and cost $750, 000 for each of the two seasons. Five to ten per cent of the mailing list "dies" every year.

As is usually the case with those who sell by mail this company gives an absolute guarantee of satisfaction or money refunded only one garment in fifty is returned for alteration or exchange. The average order is for about six dollars worth of goods.

Style is the first consideration, and the business is built on this principle. Magazine advertisements offer "leaders" at attractive prices in an effort to get orders for the leaders, and thus to establish trade relations. After this relation has once been established, catalogs are sent to the customers each season. If a customer has not ordered for two seasons, it is customary to drop her name from the list.

5. *Costs of mail-order specialty advertising.* There is no other kind of business in which returns from advertising can be so accurately checked as in the business of the mail-order advertiser. By careful tests he can find out exactly the particular size of space he can most profitably use and the particular appeal and wording of the copy that brings the greatest returns. Different sizes of space are experimented with, and the cost per inquiry and the cost per sale are carefully tabulated for each size. The space that results in the most profitable proportion between cost and returns is then adopted as the standard. Every word in the copy is carefully scrutinized. The change of a single word may mean the difference between profit and loss. When the advertiser has once found a piece of copy that results in maximum sales, he often uses the copy unchanged as long as it continues to "pull" satisfactorily.

Many mail-order specialty houses use only one-inch advertisements. Others use profitably still smaller space. A canoe manufacturer selling by mail has for several years confined his magazine copy to half-inch advertisements, finding that whenever the space was increased there was no profit in the business.

6. *Using records in choosing media.* Not only can size of space and kind of copy be standardized; the media used can also be chosen, by tests, with absolute

knowledge of their comparative usefulness to the advertiser. Those media that bring returns at a cost below the maximum set by the advertiser are continued on the list; all others are dropped.

The method of testing media is illustrated by the records of a magazine that conducted a subscription campaign by means of advertisements in a long list of magazines and newspapers. The size of space varied somewhat in different media, but both the size of space and the copy were sufficiently uniform to permit a fair comparison among the different media on the basis of the actual results recorded from the advertising in each one. Some of the tabulated results were as follows. Names of publications are not used because it would not be fair to the media to show actual results unless all the many conditions surrounding the campaign were likewise stated. Some of the media were used more than once.

	Cost of the advertisement	Number of subscriptions sold	Cost per subscription
Magazine A	$40	51	$0.79
Magazine A	40	20	2.00
Magazine B	250	338	.72
Magazine B	250	181	1.38
Magazine C	37	47	.80
Magazine D	200	234	.85
Newspaper A	12	17	.71
Newspaper B	90	258	.35

When records of this sort are continued over a long enough time and the results of various insertions in the same magazine are averaged and compared with other average returns from other media, the advertiser can definitely pick those publications that, for his particular purpose, bring the most results for the least money.

7. *Difficulties of specialty mail-order selling.* Women are said to be better mail-order buyers than men. There is a variety of suggested reasons: Some people contend that women read advertisements more carefully than men-that careful perusal of an advertisement is essential before an order will be sent by mail, and that men have less time to read carefully. Others say that men are less inclined than women to ask for their money back when they are dissatisfied with a purchase.

When a guarantee of "satisfaction or your money back" is made, a woman will ordinarily act on it if she is not satisfied, but many men will pocket their loss and give the seller no opportunity to remedy the trouble. Many men, therefore, rather than risk loss, refrain from buying by mail even when the advertiser makes a plain offer of money back in case of dissatisfaction. Other reasons also are advanced, but, whatever the reason, the seller of goods to men by mail usually has a rather difficult task.

The many attempts to sell cigars by mail have proved the necessity of great attention to details in trying to get mail orders from men. One cigar manufacturer offered "Genuine Havana Seconds" at $1.90 a box as a mail-order leader. With the goods was sent an attractive catalog illustrating forty other kinds of cigars. It was expected that the real profit would come from orders for higher-priced cigars from men who originally bought the "Havana Seconds." It was found, however, that there were only twenty five per cent of reorders, and that many of them were for the "Havana Seconds" rather than for higher-priced goods. Also, the manufacturer gradually was made to believe that many original purchasers did not like the "Havana Seconds," and that, despite the absolute offer of "money back if not set satisfactory," they neither reordered nor gave the manufacturer a chance to "make good." There seemed to be an inherent weakness somewhere in the selling plan. The problem was threefold:

1. To devise a plan which, without increasing the size of the advertisements, would increase the percentage of first orders.
2. To increase the proportion of reorders.
3. To increase the orders for higher-priced cigars than the "Havana Seconds."

The first purpose was realized by a radical change in the copy; it was given much greater attention value and told the story almost at a glance. The second and third purposes were achieved by a new offer: "To each purchaser of 100 Havana Seconds we will extend the privilege of ordering, for 60 cents additional, one of our Sample Cases containing one sample cigar each of our 12 Best Sellers—all Bargain Values—
price up to $12 per 100. Include this in your order—it's the biggest sample value we ever offered."

The sixty cents really paid the wholesale cost of the box of samples, so there was no actual loss on the transaction. The seeming attractiveness of the offer induced a large increase in orders, each one of which paid for itself no matter whether there were reorders or not; and there was a considerable increase in the percentage of reorders, most of them being for the higher priced cigars which were sent in the sample box.

8. *Selling by mail to get distribution.* When a manufacturer attempts to induce dealers to handle his goods he is often met with the statement: "We will handle your goods if you will first create a demand for them." To meet this situation, a manufacturer may decide to sell direct to consumers by mail. Then, when he can show a certain number of people who are regular users of his goods, dealers are ordinarily glad to handle them. That it is possible to create a demand thru the mails, and later to turn the business into dealer channels, is evidenced by the experience of the Lindstrom-Smith Company, of Chicago, manufacturers of vibrators and other electrical appliances.

I sold by mail-order exclusively until some years ago, when the expressed interest of the dealers became so strong that I decided to go after the dealer business in a whole-hearted fashion. Contrary to the expectation of some of my friends, the ratio between mail-order and dealer sales in my business during four years was as follows:

	Dealer	Mail-Order
1st year	25%	75%
2nd "	50%	50%
3rd "	70%	30%
4th "	80%	20%

Yet my mail-order business increased absolutely at a greater rate each succeeding year, although we refer mail-order inquiries to dealers when there is a dealer in the prospect's locality. The reason for this, I think, lies largely in the attitude we take toward the dealer. We sincerely believe that our mail-order methods are the best, if not the only possible means of "sampling" the country for the dealer's benefit.

Some manufacturers attempt to obtain dealer distribution and to do a mail-order business at the same time. Dealers in most cases do not like this. If a manufacturer who has a dealer in a community tries to induce him to push sales of the manufacturer, goods, and yet accepts direct mail orders from consumers in that community, the dealer is not to be blamed if he is not enthusiastic about the manufacturer and his product. There are two accepted methods of overcoming this difficulty. The more common is for a manufacturer who receives mail orders to ml direct orders from communities in which he has no dealers, to turn over to his retailers mail orders that come from territories in which there is a distributor. The other method is for the manufacturer to fill mail orders direct, but to give dealers their profits on business from their communities, even when the manufacturer fills the order himself. A dealer who receives a check for a transaction in which he has had no part is inclined to feel that he is overlooking a profit by not handling the manufacturer's line, and he is likely to be entirely willing to cooperate with a man who treats the trade so fairly.

9. *Department store mail-order campaigns*. As methods of transportation are improved and as the people of any trade territory gain confidence in the department stores in the large cities, these establishments find themselves more and more forced to install mail-order departments. Many of them do not carry on extensive mail-order campaigns; they accept such mail orders as come to them, but do not go out actively after mail-order business. Others use different kinds of direct advertising, and some advertise for mail orders in periodicals. A common method is to depend on the suburban circulation of newspapers to bring in orders by mail as a result of the regular newspaper advertisements.

There is difference of opinion as to whether a department store should publish regular mail-order catalog.

There are only a fewer department stores that try to do business by mail over large sections of the country. The regular department store buyers are often not competent to judge the requirements of the country trade, and, unless a special mail-order stock is maintained separate from the stock for the store, many items listed in a catalog are likely to be sold out before mail-order customers order them. Perhaps the most general practice among progressive department stores is not to carry a separate mail-order stock, nor to issue complete mail-order catalogs, but, instead, to issue frequent small bulletins of regular current store offerings, all of them subject to prior sale; or to encourage mail orders in newspaper copy, and then to build up mail-order trade by careful attention to orders when they are received.

10. *General mail-order distributors*. The campaigns of the great mail-order houses that sell almost numberless things over wide sections of the country are too well known to need much description. Most of these houses use periodicals, reaching people more or less distant from large and well-stocked stores, chiefly

for the purposes of getting the names of people to whom complete catalogs may be sent. Then these names are followed up with a great variety of attractive direct advertising matter until the prospect has become a regular customer or until his case has proved hopeless. As was shown in a previous chapter, some of the mail-order houses have grown to such tremendous proportions that there are few periodical they can profitably use to add more names to their lists.

11. *Mail order successes and failures*. The public is inclined to believe that selling by mail is easy and that there is little expense or risk in it. As a matter of fact the number of mail-order failures probably greatly exceeds the number of successes. People are so familiar with the large volume of business done by a few of the better known mail-order establishments, that many are tempted to go into the-mail. order business for themselves, without adequate, capital and without the careful preliminary study which such a business requires. In no line of selling activity is it possible to be successful without intensive investigation of the things to be sold, the people to be reached, the methods of reaching them and, above all, the probable costs of conducting the enterprise. All these things are particularly necessary in undertaking a mail-order business. Cost of doing business is the rock on which many such businesses have been wrecked. But if the risks are great, the opportunities are equally large. Hundreds of business houses, now finding a limited market for their goods, can, with proper preparation, greatly enlarged and their sales by cultivating the trade which in many cases can be quickly, safely and profitability reached thru the malls.

REVIEW

- Could a ten cent loaf of bread be sold profitably by mail? A book? A dollar razor? What considerations determine the answer to this question?
- How do the three kinds of mall-order advertising campaigns differ in purpose and method?
- Do you buy by mail? If so, what sort of things? What mail-order advertising appeals to influence you? Could you use these same appeals in advertising to others?
- Have you studied the possibility of using the mails to increase the sales of the business with which you are connected?
- Have you looked thoroughly into the matter of costs, competition, number of possible purchases, methods of reading them, etc.?

ADVISORY 16

PUBLIC SENTIMENT CAMPAIGNS

1. *A new use of advertising.*   Advertising ta mold public sentiment is new. Only recently has the world begun to understand the great power of advertising to accomplish things entirely outside the field of commerce. The public service corporation, the political party and even the government are gradually coming to realize that advertising may be perfectly dignified, that people are influenced by advertising, and that, if a cause is just, a straightforward statement over the signature of a responsible individual or company will more quickly change public sentiment than any other known means.

The most important requisite for such advertising is the same as the essential requisite of commercial advertising—there must be quality in the article advertised. The cause of the advertiser must be just. Advertising will only accelerate the failure of an organization if its product does not have quality; and advertising to create a certain public sentiment will only injure the advertiser if the judgment of the masses considers his cause unjust.

2. *The campaign versus the press agent.* Before the days of the public sentiment campaign, the press agent often was used to get free publicity. The desire of corporations, individuals, cities and political parties to mold public opinion is nothing new. Only the methods are new. Formerly it seemed to be the general opinion that it was the duty of the newspapers to give free publicity on any subject that had even the slightest claim to public interest. If a retail dealer bought a new counter, the local paper must mention it in its news columns. If the charity organization wanted funds, a carefully planned advertising campaign in space bought and not begged, was seldom thought of. If a railroad had anything to say to the public, as a

147

matter of course it told the editor to say it—and the editor usually did. At one time the use of brick as a building material was largely increased by a press agent campaign; newspapers were flooded with stories about the great loss to the country occasioned by the burning of frame structures. Hundreds of different kinds of businesses have sought to wheedle editors into telling their story, instead of buying space in the paper to tell it. The press agent still survives. Organized baseball and theaters still get tremendous amounts of free publicity. Automobiles are still "press agented" to some extent. There is scarcely a day that even the least influential editor is not urged to lend his news and editorial columns to the furthering of some private interest or some public interest backed by an active organization. The press agent still has his place; and certainly the newspapers and magazines will always devote much space to worthy causes and to matters of real public interest. But the editor is getting wary. The individual or the corporation with an axe to grind is no longer made at home in the offices of publications.

Then, too, people who wish to influence public opinion are beginning to realize that a well-displayed advertisement is likely to be seen and read by more people than the same story told in the news columns. It is this realization that has had most to do with the decreasing importance of the press agent and the increasing number and importance of real advertising campaigns designed to sell ideas instead of goods, When carefully planned advertising campaigns are paid for and carried on successfully for such movements as those represented by the National Security League and the Belgian Relief Committee, no one need hesitate to use advertising to accomplish any worthy purpose that depends for its success on the acceptance of an idea by the multitude.

3. *Political advertising campaigns.*   The Lincoln and Douglas debates in 1860 marked the end of the period when politicians relied chiefly on the human voice to sway public sentiment. Then came the era of free publicity. It is not yet at an end, but it is drawing to a close. Mark Hanna is said to have been the first political leader to buy advertising space for use in a presidential campaign. Since that time paid political advertising has greatly increased, until in the presidential campaign of 1920, it played an exceedingly important part in the activities of both the great parties.

Reliance on free publicity in a political campaign is singularly futile. Nearly every newspaper is partisan, and it is read almost entirely by members of the party with which it is affiliated. Those readers do not, ordinarily, need to be convinced of the advisability of voting for the candidate of their party. And yet free publicity for the Republican party will be received only by Republican newspapers, and free publicity for the Democrats can be inserted only in Democratic papers. The Republicans want to convince Democratic voters, and the Democrats want to convince Republicans. The only way any party organization can talk effectively in print to members of the other party is in papers read by those members; and the only way in which they can tell their story in those papers is by purchasing space in the advertising columns.

In planning a political advertising campaign it is customary now to employ trained advertising men, who study the problem just as a manufacturer studies his marketing problem. The normal vote of all parties is ascertained, the conditions affecting the probable vote in each state are charted, a study is made of the special party appeals that ought to be successful in reaching each different class of people, and the appropriation is divided among those media that will best reach the classes aimed at. Each state is given attention in proportion to its normal vote, its electoral vote and the degree of difficulty that is expected in convincing the voters. All publicity media are used.

4. *Advertising for fair play.* A gas company controlling a monopoly in a city of 350,000 population entered into an agreement with the city council allowing the council to fix rates every three years, provided only "that no rate should be so fixed as to fail to afford a fair return on the capital investment of the company."

At one of the rate-fixing periods the city council employed an expert to determine what would be a fair rate. He recommended a decrease from eighty-five to seventy cents a thousand cubic feet, maintaining that the gas company's property was worth only $4,318,178, although the company has been paying taxes on an assessed valuation of $7,078,520 which was dated by the city. Despite the apparent injustice, the council seemed determined to accept the recommendation and to establish the lower rate. It would have been impossible for the gas company to get the newspapers to present the company's case editorially, because, as the editor of one of the papers said, "If there is even the slightest suspicion these days that a newspaper is favoring a public service corporation, the cry goes up that it has 'sold out,' and half its usefulness is gone." Accordingly, the company was forced to advertise to carry its case to the people.

Full-page advertisements were used in all the papers, with daily insertions during the ten days preceding action by the council. Each advertisement was signed by the president of the company. All the advertisements formed a logical series, and yet each one stood alone as an effective presentation of the company's case. The story was told in a straightforward manner, combining the logical appeal of a lawyer with the narrative style of a newspaper story. Supplementing the newspaper advertising, a booklet was sent to every influential citizen, suggesting that he speak to his alderman if he were convinced of the justice of the company's position.

The campaign did not keep the city council from lowering the rate, but it did result in a later compromise which was satisfactory both to the citizens and to the gas company.

5. *Advertising to win strikes.* When employees of a company go out on strike, a considerable portion of the public always jumps to the conclusion that the cause of the strikers must be just and that the employer must be in the wrong. Public sentiment has a decided influence on the success or failure of a strike, particularly when a public service corporation is affected. Public sentiment can often force arbitration, or, if it is sufficiently aroused, it can bring one side or the other to speedy terms. When public sentiment is on the side of the strikers, simply because they are strikers, the employer has a difficult task to obtain a fair hearing. Free publicity in the newspapers is seldom effective, because of the popular suspicion of the disinterestedness of some editorial utterances. Therefore many employers tell their story to the people by means of an advertising campaign. Newspapers are usually employed, also posters, booklets distributed on trains, and other media are used in some instances.

Strikers use advertising to sway public sentiment less often than employers. When the influencing of public sentiment is necessary, however, there is no reason why properly planned and conducted advertising campaigns should not be used by either side in a strike controversy.

6. *Advertising for general good-will.* When a public service company has a virtual monopoly in its field, it ought to be eager to build up popular good-will, not so much to increase the immediate sale of its services, as to establish a strong foundation of popular approval which will serve as a bulwark against future competition or public hostility. All interesting campaign of this sort was undertaken in the latter part of 1916 by the Pullman Company. The company began at that time a series of

advertisements calling public attention to the various features of Pullman service, and reminding readers of the tremendous increase in the ease of traveling brought about by the developments in the equipment and in the service of the Pulhnan Company. A campaign to head off public ownership or rate regulation has been carried on for some years by the American Telephone and Telegraph Company.

Advertising alone, of course, cannot build good-will for a public service corporation any more than advertising alone can make sales. The goods and the policy of the house must be right if sales are to be made; advertising can only reflect the solid facts of quality and service. In a similar manner, a corporation can build good-will only if it deserves good-will; the advertising can only carry to a wide audience the policy of the corporation, which is reflected in its actual dealings with its patrons. It can remind the public of points in the company's service which might otherwise be forgotten, but success cannot be expected if the experience of the public does not coincide with the impression sought to be created by the advertising.

7. *Cooperative public sentiment campaigns.* Differing only in magnitude from public sentiment campaigns conducted by single corporations, is the campaign carried on by a group of interests operating cooperatively when they are confronted by the common necessity of taking their case to the people. A recent spectacular example was the effect of the leading railroads of the country, assisted by nine advertising agencies, to avert threatened labor troubles in the summer of 1916. Seventeen thousand newspapers were used to carry the railroads' case to the public. Fourteen thousand of these were weeklies reaching people in small communities.

8. *Advertising a charity.* The Great War brought out many new uses for advertising. One of the most striking of these is the charity drive which developed from raising money for what were known as War Chest Funds. Previous to that time, most city charities undertook private canvasses thru personal solicitation of certain groups of citizens. Charities became so numerous, however, that it seemed as though the solicitation for charity on an organized basis was becoming fully as much a constant nuisance as the beggar of a few centuries ago. The war developed many additional calls for money and these calls were for amounts never dreamed of before. The citizens of Cleveland, Detroit, Cincinnati, Minneapolis and many other large cities notified the charities to submit budgets and planned extensive sales campaigns to raise all of the money necessary at one time. Cleveland's first War

Chest Drive produced more than four million dollars and that figure has been repeated nearly every year since. Both sales and advertising effort are timed and every advisable medium of publicity is used.

9. *Cooperative campaigns for specific industries.* Akin to public sentiment campaigns are the campaigns conducted cooperatively by various industries to increase the consumption of the products of those industries. Among the industries that have attempted on a large scale to increase consumption have been the fruit growers, various groups of lumber interests, cement manufacturers and the producers and distributers of dairy products.

Probably the most successful and spectacular of these campaigns is the one conducted by the California Fruit Growers' Exchange. As early as 1896, this organization of growers of oranges and lemons adopted the "Sunkist" trade-mark and began to market fruit cooperatively. This organization acts as a clearing house for its members and markets the fruit at actual cost. Seventy-five branch offices were originally established in the principal cities throughout the country. These officers were in daily telegraphic touch with headquarters, and kept the home office informed of the state of the local fruit markets. They saw that shipments to each district paralleled local demand, thereby freeing the industry from the violent price fluctuations that always accompany the marketing of a perishable product when no organized attempt is made to correlate supply and demand.

When the organization was formed, California shipped about two million boxes of oranges a year and the growers thought they were over-producing. The supply was so far in excess of the demand that at times the returns were less than the cost. By 1900 the sales had been pushed up to ten million boxes and by 1917 the sales passed twenty million boxes. The advertising appropriation is somewhat in excess of one-half million dollars a year. The following table gives the business of the California Fruit Growers' Exchange and the percentage for sales and advertising expense by years from 1910 through 1919.

Year	Sales	Percentage for advertising and selling expense
1910	$14,831,975	3.57
1911	20,708,000	3.25
1912	17,235,822	3.53

1912	$13,640,091	2.62
1914	18,990,725	3.31
1915	19,628,397	3.72
1916	27,675,920	3.14
1917	33,478,130	3.01
1918	36,291,675	1.79
1919	54,627,556	2.01

It is said that the marketing cost of the California Fruit Growers' Exchange is less than that of any other commodity regardless of its nature. The success of the Exchange is a striking tribute to the value of organization backed by vigorous, persistent advertising.

10. *Advertising a city.* Campaigns to advertise cities are not strictly public sentiment campaigns. They are sales campaigns, intended to sell the city and its opportunities to factories looking for a home and to people looking for a desirable place to live in or to visit. Nevertheless, because they are conducted in the interests of groups of people instead of single individuals or companies, and because they are not concerned with the sale of merchandise, they have more in common with public sentiment campaigns than with any other kind of advertising. Some cities advertise to bring tourists. and conventions. The cities of the Pacific coast have done this to a large extent. Others wish to attract factories and to bring in permanent residents. This is a newer development in city advertising than advertising for tourist trade. Many cities have tried it—some of them in a spectacular way.

A few years ago Des Moines, as "the city of certainties," was heralded in the advertising columns of many national magazines. Magazine advertising, however, is by no means the only sort of publicity that cities use to build up the communities. There is scarcely a chamber of commerce or commercial club in the United States that has not a more or less carefully planned campaign to attract visitors, interest factory owners and bring in residents. Usually the campaign consists entirely in the use of direct media. Booklets describing the city and its advantages are the mainstay of the publicity. These booklets may be supplemented by letters, trade excursions and a variety of other things that are expected to attract attention to a community and to arouse interest in it.

The value of city advertising depends on several things. First, there must be something to advertise. Unless there are some real reasons why people should buy a certain commodity it will do no good to advertise that commodity. In like manner, a city that has no real advantages as a factory site or as a place of residence can scarcely expect to get results from advertising. The trouble with many town promotion campaigns is that there was no adequate "study of the product" before the campaign was undertaken. An analysis will often show that a town needs to "clean house" in many different ways before it can afford to set out consciously to attract attention to itself. Advertising that is better than the article advertised is as bad for a city as for a manufacturer.

Actual recorded results of city advertising campaigns are difficult to get. A few are available, however. Among them perhaps the most successful recorded results were from a campaign conducted by Nashville in 1911. Booklets were prepared; magazines and newspapers were used; and local campaigns with personal workers were carried on for short periods in the leading cities of the country. The reported expenses and results were as follows:

EXPENSES

Direct advertising (23 pieces)	$20,000
Periodical advertising	25,000
Office expense	10,000
Factory sites and assisting factories	12,000
Entertainment of conventions	14,000
Sundry expenses	17,000
TOTAL	$98,000

RESULTS

74 new factories

292 conventions

During 1919 the City of New Orleans subscribed from the Mayor's contingent fund a large sum for a nine months' advertising campaign preparatory to the convention of the Associated Advertising Clubs of the World. Double page spreads appeared in magazines, and the street cars were also used. The campaign made plain to inland communities the great advantages of the City of New Orleans as a port.

That it does not require excessive expenditures to build up a city if the city really has something to offer and the campaign is properly conducted, is indicated by the experience of Calgary, Alberta. In 1914, with an advertising expenditure of only $11,000, Calgary was successful in attracting twelve new manufacturing enterprises.

11. *Advertising a state.*   The members of the Portland Commercial Club, realizing that Portland is the largest city in Oregon, and estimating that of every dollar earned in the state sixty cents is spent in Portland, as early as 1907 developed a plan to advertise the State of Oregon and its resources. The Oregon Development Association was formed by the members of the Portland Commercial Club. Their motto is: "Not one cent to advertise Portland—everything for Oregon."

Advertisements were inserted in many periodicals in order to elicit inquiries for literature about the state. Commercial clubs were organized in all the small towns, and a bulletin was issued twice a week to these commercial clubs giving the names and addresses of inquirers, together with the specific subjects in which they appeared to be interested. The Oregon Development Association mailed a booklet and a letter to each inquirer, and each community selected from the names of inquirers certain people on whom it concentrated its efforts.

The proprietors of summer resorts and the smaller towns along the automobile routes in Minnesota have organized the Minnesota Ten Thousand Lakes Association which advertises the beauty of that state as tourist attraction. While the proprietors of the summer resorts subscribe to the campaign for the immediate business which it brings them, the bankers and other business men in the small towns find that their subscriptions are well repaid in the new business the advertising brings the community.

As an example of how this plan worked, consider the case of Creswell, Oregon. When Creswell associated itself with the campaign it was thirty-two years old, had a population of 300 and did not have a bank. A commercial club was organized, and an appropriation of $1,500 to supplement the advertising of the Oregon Development Association was subscribed. The secretary of the commercial club asked each resident to fill out a card giving the section of the East in which he had once lived or in which he had friends. These cards were arranged geographically; when a list of inquirers was received from the Oregon Development Association, the local secretary entered into correspondence only with people located in districts where the inhabitants of Creswell had friends. The secretary kept in constant telephone communication with the people in the town, and each inhabitant arranged a follow-up series of personal letters of his own to persons living near his old eastern home, who, by responding to the advertising of the Oregon Development Association, had shown an interest in the West and its opportunities. Not only would the father of the family write to the inquirer, but the children would write to the children of the inquirer, and in some cases the wife of the Oregon man would write to the wife of the Easterner telling of her experiences in Oregon, and urging the eastern woman to consider moving West and becoming a neighbor again. Thru such cooperative effort has the West been built. In two years Creswell doubled in population. The adjacent farm lands trebled in value. The new bank was a thriving institution. Concrete sidewalks were laid. New buildings went up, and the inhabitants of Creswell proved to the world that no city is too small to advertise.

12. *Advertising national needs.* Some of the most interesting uses of advertising were brought out by the great war. Before the United States entered the conflict, we had heard of the remarkable publicity thru all forms of advertising which had been used in Great Britain, in recruiting its great army.

The experience of our Ally led the United States into advertising campaigns unprecedented heretofore. Whether it was a matter of recruiting the army, navy or marines, conserving food, the sale of bonds or of War Savings Stamps, or the collection of money for the Red Cross and other war service organizations, the message was brought home to our people by advertising that flamed, it seemed, on every wall and from every window. The best advertising talent in the nation was placed at the service of the government, and every device of modern advertising was freely utilized. Not only was the advertising experience mobilized in the nation's service, but the nation's advertisers themselves were called upon for patriotic effort. To them is due the extensive newspaper advertising which characterized the war period. Central organs in Washington prepared copy and asked the national advertisers to pay for its insertions in the newspapers. The story of this advertising activity would require a volume for all the details of its achievements, but the evidence of its work was brought home to every citizen.

13. ***Modern national advertising.*** Foremost among the associations contributing to the advertising of the government during the war was the American Association of

Advertising Agencies. After the war, this association, representing in its membership the agencies which place more than 90% of all national advertising, proposed to the government a plan by which the talent of all of these agencies might be used for any advertising campaigns any of the departments of the government might undertake. A separate corporation was formed known as the Advertising Agencies Corporation. While the permanent offices of the corporation are in New York and while a regular staff for the operating department of agency service is constantly maintained, the other three steps of agency service, investigating, planning and producing, are performed by the different members on assignment. The Agencies Corporation has handled special recruiting drives for both the Army and Navy and has at different times undertaken advertising campaigns for other departments of the government.

REVIEW

- What is the first requirement of a public sentiment campaign?
- Do you believe that paid advertising on a large scale is advisable for a great exposition? Why?
- What two things can a monopoly hope to accomplish by advertising?
- When workers strike, why does the employer advertise?
- Many city advertising campaigns fail. Why?
- Can you think of things the United States government might accomplish by advertising, other than those mentioned in the chapter?

ADVISORY 17

THE TRADER'S CAMPAIGN

1. *Classes of distributors*. The campaigns thus far considered are essentially those of the manufacturer. The special advertising problems of the distributor remain to be considered. Here the usual distinction between the wholesaler or jobber on the one hand, and the retailer on the other is significant for our purpose since each has his special needs.

Sometimes indeed we hear of an advertiser who is both manufacturer and jobber. So far as he is a manufacturer his problems have already been considered; so far as he is a jobber his special needs will be discussed in the sections which follow.

2. *Development of jobber advertising*. Publicity by jobbers is of comparatively recent date. In former days a few announcements appeared in the trade papers. But when the dealer paid for his insertions be reckoned it as an act of kindness to the publisher, as means of securing good-will, sometimes perhaps as a tribute exacted to prevent ill-will, and did not count it as a part of any well defined policy for increasing the sale of his goods. In recent years dealer advertisements have become more numerous and more extensive.

Formerly the advertisements of different jobbers were as like as two peas. The firm name and a notice of the line it dealt in, often embellished with a cut of its office, warehouse or trade symbol formed the sum and substance of jobber advertising. More recently there has been an effort toward greater variety.

A variation from traditional forms came in the endeavor to exploit jobbers' private brands. Any campaign to push a special commodity or group of commodities will of course follow the same methods whether it is a manufacturer or a jobber who foots the bill. What these methods are has already been discussed. How far the jobber may be justified in this special expenditure for a limited part of his stock is a question to be decided in each particular case.

After all comparatively few jobbers believe it to be profitable to advertise their own private brands, and this is not the predominant form of jobber advertising. Most jobbers handle competing lines and prefer to emphasize the variety and quality of their stock, and especially the service which they can render to their customers. They believe that the retailer is interested not so much in any particular brand of goods as in getting what he wants, and getting it promptly. Thru his advertising as well as thru his other sales efforts, the jobber seeks to impress as forcefully as possible on the retailer that he can render the latter real service.

3. *Jobber's gain thru advertising.* While modern business emphasizes the idea of service, it does not go so far as to confuse service with philanthropy. The jobber makes no pretense that he offers exceptional service to the retailer out of pure goodness of heart. His advertising bears a definite relation to his own business policy. It is designed of course to build up good-will, but it serves another important function in paving the way for the sales force. Advertising is an effective adjunct to the work of the sales force, particularly when a new product or a new line is taken up by the house.

4. *Media for the jobber.* The jobber's market is in some respects a limited one. He appeals not to the general public but to the retail merchants who are in his line of business and who are within the area of his operations. He has little if anything to gain by going beyond the special trade papers for general publicity. But here again he must be on his guard against waste circulation. He pays for wasted effort if the paper selected circulates widely outside the area he serves. He wastes money when he advertises in journals of poor quality or limited circulation. In the one instance he reaches persons whose trade he may esteem of little value. In the other he fails to reach as many as he should.

The difficulties which attend trade paper publicity often lead jobbers to make an extensive use of the various forms of direct advertising.

5. *Retailer's advertising.* While the jobber seeks to reach a special public in a comparatively large area, the retailer directs his efforts to the general public in a much restricted area. This fundamental difference in purpose dominates the advertising as well as other sales efforts of the retailer. His service is directly to the consumer and this fact must guide his advertising policy. Furthermore the many and varied types of business which are included under the general term retailer and the necessities of different lines of business dictate different advertising methods according to circumstances. Two retailers even in the same line may employ entirely different methods and yet both be successful.

6. *What is advertising.* It may seem late in the day to raise the question, what is advertising, but it has a direct bearing upon the retailer's needs. The purpose of retail advertising is sometimes said to be to get people to the store and to induce them to buy. Retail trade offers so many points of personal contact between buyer and seller, that when advertising is thus defined it may readily be stretched to include all means of securing attention and all sales inducements. In a certain broad sense a store advertises thru its sign, its store front, its window dressing, its interior displays, and the conveniences which it offers the public.

In a general way we may distinguish between inducements to visit the store and inducements to purchase, It is the former group of activities—the long range operations, as it were—that are distinctively advertising and obviously nothing else. It is to them that the present discussion is limited.

7. *An advertising policy.* We are concerned here with advertising campaigns, the complete and definite expression of an advertising policy which has been determined upon. The small retailer, more perhaps than any other class, has very hazy ideas as to the value of advertising, and is often fickle, haphazard, and therefore ineffective in the expenditure which he makes for that purpose. No matter how small the business unit, it should adopt a definite attitude and policy with regard to advertising. The retailer may conclude that in his business no advertising would be profitable, but if he reaches such a conclusion then let him at least hold to it until he has tried out the policy for a sufficient length of time to test its value. Whatever the policy may be it should be so firmly fixed in his own mind that he can withstand the wiles of the solicitors who very often offer him nothing for something.

In retail trade as elsewhere, there is a distinct advantage in having a definite advertising appropriation and a definite plan for spending it. One feature of such a plan will of necessity be its regularity. Regularity, it may be noted, need not imply monotony. Variety is an essential of effective publicity. Regularity will, however, combat the prejudice which exists in the minds of many retailers that it only pays to advertise when they have some "special sale."

Progressive retailers are beginning to realize that this is a delusion. Advertising of such a nature is perhaps the least profitable form which the retailer can adopt. Better advertising is that which directs the attention of possible purchasers to the regular stock which is sold at the regular prices, and arouses interest in these goods. No retailer who adopts a definite and regular advertising policy will succumb to the widely prevalent delusion that every advertisement should pay for itself, and do it quickly. He will not expect the returns from advertising to be immediately discernible. He will understand that a particular advertisement may be felt weeks and even months after its insertion. The purpose of advertising is to create good-will for the house and even though immediate results can not be discovered, it is not necessarily wasted. The salesman on the road may be disappointed in not getting an order from one of his customers, but he does not necessarily feel that his call has been entirely fruitless. In many cases, to the contrary, he knows that he has made it easy to effect a sale on his next call. In other words, he has made an investment in good-will from which he may reasonably expect dividends in the future. This should also be the attitude of the advertiser. He should remember that persistence in good work brings its reward.

8. *What makes poor copy.* There is probably no field in which advertising is more hackneyed and more perfunctory than in the notices inserted in the smaller papers by average retail dealers. Many of them are content with an announcement of the firm's name, the goods dealt in and the location of the store. In inserting such notices some delude themselves into the belief that they are advertising, while others who know no other kind of copy have been cured of the delusion and have adopted a new one that "advertising does not pay." If a retailer imagines that his notice in the paper serves no purpose other than that of a classified business directory of telling people what persons and firms in town deal in certain articles, he had better leave advertising alone and save his money.

The wrong kind of advertising never pays, the right kind always does. It is the merchant's problem to determine what is the right kind for him. This of course will depend on a wide variety of circumstances. In any case there are general rules to guide him.

9. **What makes good copy.** To make good copy and to obtain the purpose for which it is designed, the retailer's advertisement must have vim, vigor, interest and personality.

Wishy-washy, spineless statements attract no attention. The reader passes them by. Vigorous, direct and forceful language in an advertisement compels people to read who had no thought of doing so when picking up the paper. While this is true, no one is pleasantly impressed by mere noise. The beating of tin pans is never agreeable. There must be something back of it. This something is the story which the advertiser has to tell.

The story must be interesting. The advertiser can well take his cue from the reading matter in the paper. He knows that however curious and informing may be the patent insides which are the delight of mural journalism, after all people in his community are most keenly interested in the news of the day. Therefore he should make his advertisement deal with store news. If he adopts this plan he will not allow his material to grow stale, for he will know that as soon as it becomes musty it is no longer news, and no longer of interest. This means that advertising must change frequently, bring out new features of merchandise and service, and if he can educate his public to say instinctively, and some advertisers have accomplished this, "I wonder what (blank) says today," or "this week," he will have attained the highest goal.

The personality in one's advertising should be distinctive. The example of the great department stores might well be followed by other advertisers. In large cities the newspaper reader recognizes certain advertisements even at a distance, as belonging to certain stores. There is a distinctive use of type, borders, illustrations and arrangement which gives to the advertising of such stores a definite personality. This is an element in attracting and holding attention which is not to be neglected.

10. **Types of retail advertising.** Advertising by retailers varies with the different kinds of goods which they offer for sale. But more important variations result

from the several types of stores included under the general designation of retailer. The small store whether it be a general country store or a specialty store, must meet different conditions from the chain stores on the one hand and the department stores on the other. These conditions are again modified by the location of the small store, whether it is in a small community or in the midst of a great city.

11. *Small store advertising.* The typical small store in smaller communities is not given to advertising. The proprietor usually feels that everybody in town knows who he is, where he is and what he sells. Of what use then to constantly force himself on the attention of the public? It is a comparatively small mind that thinks in this way. Such a man probably deceives himself. Some people know him but it is a question whether everybody does, and it is a still greater question whether everybody is interested in the service which he can render. No excellence of his goods or his service can bring his enterprise and his wares to the active attention of so large an interested circle as can be reached thru advertising of the right sort.

12. *Choice of media.* Because the small store usually serves a comparatively limited area the retailer must exercise great discretion in the choice of advertising mediums in order to avoid waste. Newspaper publicity in large cities and in many of medium size would cost too much and would be comparatively useless to purchase. In smaller towns where distances to be covered are not great, local dealers can make effective use of the regular newspaper press.

Moreover in the larger cities there are often newspapers, usually weeklies or semi-weeklies, devoted to the use, of one section and these may serve as advertising mediums for the small merchant. He may also find it to his advantage to utilize local church papers, lodge and fraternity papers, theatre programs and the like, though these should be weighed very carefully both as respects the actual circulation which they secure and also as to the regularity of the service which they can render.

The difficulties which have been noted above have led many small stores to obtain an effective substitute rule for newspaper advertising thru the publication of store papers. In them we find a judicious mixture of news, chiefly of a local nature, and the advertising of the store which issues the paper. Such papers are in some respects akin to direct advertising, but as a rule they are not sent to definite mailing lists, but are distributed by hand thru the neighborhood which the store expects to serve.

The different forms of direct advertising by mail are used by many small stores. Circular letters to customers and prospects are often employed. Other concerns adopt the plan of sending a small folder advertising their goods at regular intervals.

13. *Chain store advertising.* The chain store is one of the most recent forms of retail selling and has had an almost phenomenal development. Chain store management has up to the present made but little use of advertising. Chain store advertising depends upon the kind of articles sold and the type of chain represented, whether national or local. Advertising methods followed by a shoe chain in which the product was sold to the consumer in stores operated by the manufacturer in a large number of cities would not serve a grocery chain which bought from jobbers and which operated in a narrow territory. With the exception of a cigar chain and a few other chains of national scope, chain stores advertise, if they advertise at all, only locally. The fact that these stores are widely dispersed throughout the community makes it possible for them to utilize metropolitan newspapers without the loss which would accrue to the usual small store in buying space in such media.

14. *Featuring of price.* Perhaps if there is any distinctive point in chain store advertising it lies in the emphasis on low prices. These cut price appeals are often supplemented by trading stamps, coupons, premium offers, and other advertising devices of a similar nature.

On the other hand chains which are established to market a specific product, such as the shoe chains, do not feature price to the same extent but make their appeal on the basis of quality, style or comfort.

15. *Advertising methods.* In short, national advertising is applicable to a few chains, but not to the great majority of them.

Most of them are local chains which until recently have used very little newspaper publicity. Theirs is strictly a neighborhood business and in the main they have relied upon the same methods of attracting trade as their independent competitors. The standardized store front of the more familiar chains may be advertising as we are using the term here, but it is a powerful magnet to attract attention and draw trade. Newspapers are used by the drug chains especially to advertise their "one cent sales." Chains also use the papers to introduce new articles. In general the amount of their newspaper advertising is small. As chains operate on a cash basis they rarely have lists of customers to whom they can appeal by direct mail advertising. A certain amount of neighborhood advertising is done thru store papers and dodgers.

16. *Department store advertising.* The department store is a product of city growth. It is a local institution with a local patronage. Its advertising is limited in its appeal to the city and its environs and in the very large cities to the metropolitan area or district. In this respect the department store is like most chain stores and other retail stores in being a local advertiser. On the other hand its trade is not a neighborhood trade, and it is not restricted in its advertising by this consideration.

17. *Choice of media.* Department store advertising is done almost exclusively thru the newspapers.

The occasional use of car cards or bill boards involves no great expenditure compared with the sums paid for newspaper advertising. Department stores are indeed greater newspaper advertisers than any other business and an important support of the business end of the newspapers. Their expenditures are enormous. In 1913, nine large department stores located in Boston, New York and Philadelphia are reported to have spent $3,700,000 on newspaper advertising. For the stores forming the group, the sums so spent were from two to five per cent of their total annual sales.

In making such general use of the newspaper to the exclusion of other media, advertising managers of department stores believe that they have secured the quickest, most accessible and most effective way of gaining publicity for their goods. No other medium can give publicity to as large a number of people in such limited time as the newspaper. Nor can a more effective way for presenting advertising news be devised.

18. *Methods of appeal.* The object of department store advertising is to induce people to come to the store, for at least a certain proportion of those who do so will become purchasers. The advertisements are prepared by specialists and set

forth in a specific way information about the style, quality and price of the goods on sale.

Like the average chain store the department store features price as one form of appeal. One phase of this appeal, the bargain sale, is fast passing into disuse or was doing so until the readjustment of retail prices that began in 1920 and temporarily, at least, made bargain sales imperative for all. Formerly a large part of department store business was built up on bargain advertising. Among the pretexts given for bargain sales were fires, overstocked goods, failures and "seconds." Normally the better kind of department store has little faith in them. Their "pull" is doubtful. A trade paper recently said: "Advertising of bargains is still printed, but the public is almost as impervious to them as the side of a battleship would be to the fire of a battery of pea shooters. The delusion still exists among many merchants that this is not so, but no such delusion exists among great merchants." This refers to the period before 1920.

Many prominent department store advertisers make their appeal on the merit of their goods. Some writers call this regular advertising, as distinguished from bargain sale advertising. Regular advertising is based on the idea that people require certain goods and that they are willing to pay a fair price for them. Advertisements, therefore, should set forth the merits of these goods in such an attractive fashion that a natural desire for them will be created. This represents a real and scientific endeavor to supply goods to people who want them, while the bargain sale method is suspected of attempting to induce persons to buy goods they do not want.

REVIEW
- What is it that the jobber should seek to impress upon the retailer through advertising?
- Why is the trade paper the best medium for jobber advertising? Why are the national magazines the poorest medium?
- Show where the average retail advertiser fails to get the most out of his advertising budget.
- Outline an advertising campaign for a small retailer in a town of 50,000 population. Write some sample copy and also indicate the media you would select and suggest the other kinds of copy you would use.

- How do the advertising campaigns conducted by chain stores and those of local department stores differ?

ADVISORY 18

THE CAMPAIGN AS A WHOLE

1. *Final problems of the advertiser.* At the conclusion of our study of advertising campaigns there remain three important things to be considered. They are not all closely related, but for convenience they are grouped together in a final chapter. The first of these three subjects is the necessity of altering the plans for a campaign from time to time, as unexpected conditions develop, or as results from the original plans dictate a realignment of the advertising forces so as to insure success of the advertiser. The second subject is a study of the several ways of binding together all the various forces in a campaign. And the last is a small group of universal advertising laws that must constantly be borne in mind by everyone who hopes to build business with the aid of advertising.

2. *Changing the plan to bring results.* It is evident to anyone who studies the variety of problems that have to be solved by the man who prepares a plan for an advertising campaign, that no plan is infallible. There are few definite rules of procedure. In only a small minority of instances can an advertiser say, "This is what I must do because experience has proved it to be the best thing to do." But no amount of study can guard against errors in human judgment. some plans for campaigns are sure to be wrong, no matter how carefully they have been made.

The possibility of a mistake in judgment makes it necessary for the advertiser to keep on the watch constantly for indications that his campaign is not doing what is was intended to do. If results do not come, if expenses amount alarmingly, if new competition develops, or if any one of many other things happen, it is time for the advertiser to take his plans apart, find the weak point and bolster it up if possible, or if something fundamental is wrong, to discard the old plans entirely and start off afresh on a new track.

3. *A selling plan that was wrong.*   The campaign of the Review of Reviews Company to sell the Photographic History of the Civil War some years ago illustrates admirably the necessity that often arises of changing a plan for a campaign after the campaign is under way. The Photographic History was a set of books containing reproductions of photographs actually taken during the Civil War. The peculiar nature of the books offered unusual advertising opportunities. Large space was taken in magazines and newspapers and the copy was excellent. An elaborate follow-up was prepared. The advertising campaign began almost before the books were ready for the market, and continued on a large scale for more than a year. The periodical advertising was not intended to make sales; inquiries only were sought, by means of a coupon in each advertisement. It was expected that the follow-up would close the sales.

The coupons came in by the thousands, the follow-up was set to work, and results eagerly awaited. Many sales were made, but they were slow in coming. At first this did not greatly trouble the publishers. The man in charge was experienced in the selling of books by mail. He did not expect immediate results, because he realized it takes time to turn inquiries into sales without the use of salesmen. Furthermore, he knew that many people would not even send in a coupon until the cumulative effect of the advertising had time to influence them.

Feeling sure that only time was necessary to make the carefully planned campaign show results, the manager went on a vacation for a few weeks. When he returned, instead of finding that sales were materializing in satisfactory volume, he found only an average selling cost of thirty dollars a set, which was the total price paid by the consumer. Something had to be done, and done quickly. Printers' Ink describes the way in which the problem was solved:

There was nothing serious the matter with the copy, for inquiries were coming in steadily. The follow-up was complete and elaborate, and was being sent out promptly. But something manifestly was wrong, for the number of those who had sent in coupons but hadn't ordered the books was increasing at a stupendous rate. Since the magazine copy seemed to be above reproach, the trouble must be in the follow-up, and careful analysis located it. The follow-up was interesting, it was artistic, it was well written, but it failed to give the inquirer an adequate impression of the size and comprehensiveness of the edition. It stimulated desire for the books, but not to the extent of thirty dollars' worth. It was instantly recognized that the only way to "cash in" on cumulative effect

169

was to give the people the opportunity to see the books themselves, since in this way only could they be convinced of the full value of the goods.

The entire edition was turned over in November to John Wanamaker and the advertising continued under the name of the Wanamaker Book Club. The books were conspicuously displayed in the store, and an easy payment plan of purchase was inaugurated. The results were immediately apparent, and the profits arrived on schedule. During the first twenty days of April, the sales aggregated five-elevenths of the total sales during the entire campaign. In other words, out of a total sale of some forty thousand sets, nearly half were sold during the last twenty days. Of course there is nothing to prove that the results would not have come if the course originally followed had been adhered to, but the probabilities are strongly against it. What made the difference between success and probable failure was the disposition to find out what was really the matter.

4. *Adapting campaign to local conditions.* An advertising and selling plan seldom has to be changed entirely after it has once been undertaken. Often, however, it must be adjusted in some minor way to meet changed conditions. Usually the adjustment involves added sales activity at some points and rearranged plans for local advertising at other points. The general plans for an advertising and sales campaign may be justified by the general business conditions in the country, and yet the varying conditions in different localities may make necessary a rapid shift in some of the attempts to link up national advertising with intensive work on dealers and consumers in individual towns.

There are many sources of information for the advertiser who wants to keep in close touch with local business conditions to the end that he may spend his money in the places where it is most needed and where it will do the most good. Chief reliance is ordinarily placed on the reports of salesmen. If salesmen are trained observers, valuable information can be obtained from them about the business of the merchants in the towns they visit. Such information should be carefully weighed, however; some salesmen are inclined to report conditions poor, as an excuse for small sales, or because in their own line things are generally slow, when other lines are not affected.

The commercial agencies can be of great help in picturing business conditions in different sections of the country. The advertiser who tries to get inquiries or to make sales by mail can often ascertain conditions in different localities by comparing returns from these advertisements, place by place and month by month.

5. *Unifying the campaign.* An advertising campaign is deserving of the name only when all parts of it work together for a common end, and when they are so related that there is no conflict, no lack of harmony, but simply a smoothly running piece of sales machinery with a definite function and a definite place for each cog and each wheel. Advertising has suffered in the past because of the failure to give a common characteristic to all the publicity of a given advertiser, and because of a lack of appreciation of the fact that advertising and sales must be closely coordinated if there is to be maximum efficiency and minimum waste. The careful advertiser gives his attention to four problems in coordination. (1) He sees to it that all his advertising has an individuality that binds the whole together into a single effective sales weapon. (2) He makes sure that his salesmen believe in his advertising and that they work with it instead of against it. (3) He shows dealers (if he sells thru dealers) how to tie up their own store display and their own newspaper advertising to his efforts to bring consumers into their stores. (4) He organizes his own factory and office so as to insure that every member of his organization personifies the spirit and policy of his publicity. The first of these problems in coordinating the parts of the campaign was considered in detail in Chapter IV.

6. *"Selling" the advertising to the salesmen.* Many salesmen do not understand the purpose and the methods of advertising. Sometimes they suspect that the increasing importance of advertising means the decreasing importance of the salesman. It is necessary, therefore, for the advertiser to be sure that his salesmen not only understand the function of advertising in general, but also that they are fully in sympathy with the purposes of his own publicity.

This attitude of some salesmen toward advertising is not unnatural. In the past, the advertising man has not been a part of the sales organization; he frequently made his plans without consulting the sales department. Under this illogical arrangement the salesmen often were not told of the advertising plans in advance; they did not know what advertising was to be done until they saw the advertisements themselves or until dealers called attention to them. Naturally the salesmen resented being left out of the plans; their lack of knowledge of the activities of the house reflected adversely on them and on their employer. The modern executive avoids these unfortunate conditions, either by putting personal salesmanship and advertising under the supervision of the Same man, or by insisting that all advertising plans be worked out in cooperation with the sales department, and by taking steps to see that the salesmen are told about the advertising, that they believe in it and use it in every possible way to increase their sales.

Advertising is "sold" to salesmen in a variety of ways. At sales conventions it is customary to have the advertising manager explain in detail the plans of the coming season, to answer questions, and to obtain the enthusiastic cooperation of the salesmen. House organs are often used to tell the men about the advertising, to explain the purpose of it and to show them how the salesmen can make the most of it. Some advertisers go so far as to explain in detail to salesmen, thru the house organ, the reasons why the different advertising mediums are used.

The most common method of keeping the salesmen in touch with the advertising is to send copies of advertisements to the men in the field for their own information, and also to help them in explaining the campaign to dealers.

The tactful advertising manager is often able to ask advice from salesmen, and to retain their interest and cooperation by showing them the reasons for his conclusions, even if he finds it necessary to reject their suggestions.

7. *"Selling" the advertising to dealers.* When goods are distributed thru dealers, there is bound to be waste in the advertising unless dealers are familiar with it and use it in every possible way to increase the sale of the advertiser's goods. It was pointed out in Chapter XVI that the dealer's cooperation cannot be expected unless the advertised goods are of good quality and carry a satisfactory profit for him. If these conditions are fulfilled, then efforts should be made to tie up the dealer and the advertising in such a way that one will supplement the other. Dealers should be informed of the advertising that is to appear. This information may come either by mail or thru the salesmen. Salesmen often carry portfolios showing future advertisements, schedules of media, circulation of media by states and by towns, and other information designed to interest the dealer in the campaign and to enable him to coordinate his sales efforts with the local and national advertising of the manufacturer. Then, just before any advertisement is to appear, the dealer receives a reminder from the manufacturer. In this way the dealer can arrange to make a display of the goods to take advantage of the advertising, or he can advertise under his own name, in the papers or by signs in his window, that he is the distributor for the advertised goods. Another method of linking up the dealer and the national advertising is to furnish the dealer with cuts that are similar to the ones used in the manufacturer's advertising.

8. *Putting the organization behind the campaign.* An advertising campaign is the expression of the advertiser's sales policy. It is his most important way of talking to the public and of telling them about himself and his goods. But it is not the only way. Every letter that goes out from a business establishment advertises that establishment. It creates a good or a bad impression, and the bad impression may be so bad that no amount of general advertising can remove it. Every time an employee of a business house comes into contact with the public he helps or he hurts his employer. No matter how casual may be the personal contact between visitors and employees of the store, office or factory, every time there is any personal contact the visitor receives a good or a bad impression of the house that the employee represents. The factory can nullify thousands of dollars' worth of advertising by failing to turn out satisfactory goods, by failing to take proper care of orders, by failing to make prompt deliveries and by failing to do many other things which good service demands.

It is not a difficult matter to tell the public about high ideals, courteous service, careful attention to orders, good products and honest treatment, but it is often a very difficult matter to be sure that every employe of the advertiser lives up to the spirit and policy behind the advertising. The advertiser who fails to see that all the members of his internal and sales organization are imbued with his ideals and that they do their best to back up the advertising, is failing in a very important respect in coordinating the various things that go to make up a successful advertising campaign.

One advertiser says, "I want every one of my advertisements to be so written that, when they are shown to my employees, everyone in my plant from the office boy to the most skilled engineer will feel a pride in the organization." He realizes that no matter how good may be the quality of the raw material, the quality of the finished product depends on the skill and intelligence of the labor, and skill and intelligence will be exercised to the degree that the workers take pride in their tasks. There are many instances in which the spirit of an organization has been greatly improved by inspiring in the employees the desire to live up to the spirit and promises of the advertising.

9. *Two fundamental laws of advertising.* There are two basic laws which every advertising man should understand and apply to his advertising campaign. While both have already been referred to in a general way, we have left a detailed

discussion of them for the last chapter, so they may have the emphasis that they deserve. The first is a law of economics; the second is a law of psychology. The first is the law of diminishing returns. The second is the law of repetition and cumulative effect. In a sense they are two balancing forces. They are to advertising what centrifugal and centripetal force respectively are to physics. The first limits the advertiser. The second and provides him with his opportunity.

10. *The point of diminishing returns.* The fundamental law of diminishing returns applies to advertising as well as to agriculture or any other industry. While in agriculture the quantity of product diminishes per unit of capital and labor, in advertising this diminution is in the value of the product.

Doubtless there are few advertisers who could not, by increasing their advertising budget, increase the number of inquiries or sales. But, after a certain point has been passed, they cannot do this except at an increased cost per inquiry or sale. For example, one advertisement might bring in 1,000 inquiries; two advertisements, 3,000 inquiries; three advertisements might even bring in 10,000 inquiries. But this proportionate increase in the number of inquiries over advertisements cannot go on indefinitely. At some point the number of inquiries per advertisement must decline, Although the total number of inquiries may continue to increase. This is the point of diminishing returns, and the employment of additional advertisements will bring about a decrease in the percentage of profit on the investment.

The sales department is subject to the same law. Every time you add a salesman to your payroll you have to add an additional expense for supervision—an additional expense in teaching that salesman how to drive in the team with the other salesmen. A business man who is his own salesman requires no supervision. When he adds another man to help him sell, he is required to spend part of his time supervising the sales of the other man and teaching him the business. When he has added four or five salesmen, he finds that they require so much supervision that he is compelled to give up selling himself, and to spend all his time supervising and directing the efforts of his salesmen in order to develop proper team work.

Then as the business grows, there comes a time when there is no possibility of increased sales in the immediate neighborhood; in order to develop, the business must branch out into new fields. This calls for traveling expenses for salesmen, which perhaps doubles the former sales expense without bringing anything like proportionate returns. The point of diminishing returns has been reached.

Thus it is with all business. As supervision and territory are added, expenses increase faster than returns. Even volume ultimately reaches a limit. There comes a point when the amount of additional expense required is exactly equal to the return that will be received. This is the point of diminishing returns. Beyond this point it is unprofitable to proceed. If it were not for this law, the fact that an advertising expenditure of $1,500,000 brought the Procter and Gamble Company $83,000,000 worth of business, might persuade the company to spend $3,000,000 or $6,000,000 in advertising the coming year on the theory that the increased expenditure would bring $166,000,000 or $332,000,000 worth of business.

Every advertising campaign has before it a point of diminishing returns. It is farther away in some businesses than in others. When there is a strong element of "repeat" in an article, the point of diminishing returns may be far in the future.

Indications that a business is approaching the point of diminishing returns may be found in the steady rise of the cost per inquiry and the steady rise of the cost per sale. The day when increased expenditure will not bring adequate returns may be postponed in some cases. The field of operations may be extended, or new products may be added which will carry prestige already established and which can be sold without much additional sales expense. But if progress continues, the point of diminishing returns is bound to be reached sooner or later in every business. That increased expenditure for advertising cannot continually bring increased returns is no indictment of the power of advertising. It is a fundamental law of economics.

11. *Cumulative effect of repetition.* The second of the two laws of advertising that we are considering has a direct bearing on the necessity of coordinating all the parts of an advertising campaign. It rests on two laws of human nature. The first says: "Attention and interest cannot be maintained except momentarily on a stimulus that remains absolutely the same." There must be something new and changing about it. The reader can, of course, voluntarily force his attention for a brief period on an advertisement but such attention cannot be continued long unless the object reveals some suggestion or idea that is of new interest to him.

The other law states: "Attention and interest cannot be maintained on a stimulus which is absolutely without meaning—a stimulus of which the reader has had no previous cognizance." We must have some link with a past experience by which we can compare a present experience, or else we immediately lose interest.

Everything that holds our attention and interest must have two elements—an element of the old and an element of the new—an element of repetition and an element of novelty. The most engrossing and interesting experiences are new experiences in old surroundings or old experiences in new surroundings. If the experiences and surroundings are both new we lose interest, just as we tire if the experiences and surroundings are both old and have become commonplace to us. Our continued interest in any object depends partly on our familiarity and association with that object, and these in turn depend on repeated contact with it.

It is the same with advertisements as with anything else that claims our attention. We welcome the advertisements of Ivory Soap and Cream of Wheat as old friends. No two of them are quite the same, and yet there is something about every one that causes ready recognition and that induces growing interest led good-will. The advertiser should strive to make the reader regard his advertisements as he regards his friends. We expect a friend always to have the same color of hair, the same features, the same height and the same mannerisms. These things remain constant, but other things about him change. He does not always wear the same clothing. He does not always talk about the same things. If he is a friend worth having, he is likely to bring to you some new idea every time you meet him. Each contact with him develops better understanding. If his ideas are always good, his manner always pleasant, his sincerity always evident: each meeting will add to your respect for him; and the more you respect him, the more willing you will be to act on his suggestions. So it is with advertisements. Their success depends largely on their persistence, on the readiness with which the reader recognizes them, and on the amount of respect that be is made to feel for the advertiser and the advertiser's goods.

12. *The family resemblance of advertisements.* A noted psychologist once said: "It is the generic family resemblance that some of the great national advertisers adhere to in their advertisements which gives the cumulative inheritance of power." Many advertisers are unable to comprehend this principle. There is no coordination in their advertising campaigns. Their advertisements inherit no power from their predecessors. Their advertisements do not look alike. But above this,

their advertisements are not so constructed as to transmit any power. They urge one thing today and another thing tomorrow. In the advertisements of today they make claims which they contradict or prove false in the statements they make tomorrow. They have no consistency either in appearance or purpose. They live from hand to mouth. It is these advertisers who most quickly find the point of diminishing returns. They are building not on a solid foundation but on sand.

The first way to give advertisements that subtle something which we call character and which the psychologist calls generic family resemblance is to build them on fundamental business policy. Many organizations do not know that they have business policies until they begin to prepare advertisements. There are certain policies of honesty and fair dealing which should be fundamental with any organization. There are other policies of trade developed with experience. Each year new policies develop or changes are needed in old ones. Each year the far-sighted employer sets down the policies of his organization and endeavors to express them in his advertising campaign.

The other method of obtaining and retaining character in all the advertisements of a campaign is in the physical make-up. This, too, may change from year to year, just as a man may change his style of dress as he grows older. It is not to be supposed that one concern will use the same style of border or the same type in all its advertisements year in and year out. But there should be something which carries the reader's mind from advertisement to advertisement—something which provides the connecting link between present and past experience, while offering opportunity for the constant change that is necessary to hold attention.

Perhaps you know a man who always wears a broad-brimmed felt. The wearing of that hat is a part of his personality. When you think of him you think of the hat. They seem to belong together. Other men, possibly, wishing to emulate him, wear the same sort of hat. Their efforts are incongruous. Instead of adopting the distinguishing outward characteristic of another individual, they should wear the hat that best merges into their own peculiarities of face, stature and character. So it is with advertisements. The physical make-up as well as the message of the advertisement must represent the character of the advertiser and his organization.

Advertising is expression. It is more than words on paper. Advertisements are the representatives of the organizations paying for them. They should be like those organizations, look like them, live like them. A truly successful advertising campaign is not developed by formula. It is an expression of character. And in so far as that character is strong, as that character is steadfast, as that character is true, to that extent, and to that extent only, may the campaign be expected to succeed.

REVIEW

- Specifically what is meant by coordinating all the parts of an advertising campaign? If you were planning a campaign, what different problems in coordination would you have to solve? How would you solve them in your business?

- How can advertising react on the advertiser and his employes?

- Why cannot increased investments in advertising continue indefinitely to bring profitable business?

- Do you believe in the business-building power of honest, consistent, persistent, interesting, attractive advertising? Could it be profitably used in the business with which you are connected? Many businesses have entered new eras of development after giving careful consideration to this question.